Dead in Good Company

A Celebration of
Mount Auburn Cemetery

Dead in Good Company

A Celebration of Mount Auburn Cemetery

Edited by John Harrison
and Kim Nagy

ZIGGY OWL PRESS
MEDFORD, MASSACHUSETTS

http://www.DeadInGoodCompany.com

Copyright

Dead in Good Company: A Celebration of Mount Auburn Cemetery

ISBN-13: 978-0996374705

Front cover photo by John Harrison.
Rear cover photos by Kim Nagy.
All photos were taken at Mount Auburn Cemetery.
Book design and production by Steve Gladstone.
www.StevesTravelGuide.com.

Praise for *Dead in Good Company*

"Like the tom turkey I once watched scratching in the Mount Auburn leaf litter, I too come here to scratch below the surface to find sustenance. Visit Mount Auburn Cemetery. Let yourself slow down and listen. Perhaps you'll hear (or at least sense) the whispers of great lives past and animal spirits present. *Dead in Good Company* gives us a peek through the Mount Auburn keyhole, allowing intimate views – diffracting, shimmering and glittering. Words and images of visitors devoted to the lives and details of the place offer a refreshing tonic from well-visited ground. Every metropolis should be so lucky to have its own Sweet Auburn – and a book that so deftly serves up its mysteries."

– Mark Wilson, wildlife journalist, chapter author and contributing photographer for *Artic Wings: Birds Of The Arctic National Wildlife Refuge*

****

"On rare and wonderful occasions, a book comes along that captures the full essence of a place – the splendor of its natural beauty, the exquisiteness of its mystery, the depth of its character. *Dead in Good Company* is such a work, revealing in powerful words and marvelous pictures the full glory of Mount Auburn Cemetery. This book whispers in some places, cries out in others; it draws you in with nuance and stuns you with resplendence. And throughout, it is a paean to the enduring treasure that is Mount Auburn. *Dead in Good Company* deserves a place on your bookshelf and in your heart."

– Stephen Puleo, author of *Dark Tide: The Great Boston Molasses Flood of 1919* and *The Caning: The Assault That Drove America to Civil War*

****

"Like the paths that wind through the lush groves, quiet grottos and rolling meadows of Boston's legendary Mount Auburn Cemetery, the stories in *Dead in Good Company* meander through time and history, both human and natural. Like a good cemetery, they encompass the range of experience, touching on architecture, Civil War reenactment, assassination, death at sea, a mother's kiss. And the thread that ties all these strands together is Sweet Auburn's wild creatures, especially its birds – the colorful spring migrants that fill its trees, the coyotes and foxes slipping like ghosts among the mausoleums, frogs in the marshes, owls in the night, and red-tailed hawks perched like sentinels on the highest monuments. In prose, poetry and stunning photography, *Dead in Good Company* shows how a place of death is, in every important way, a place of vivid, vibrant life."

– Scott Weidensaul, author of *Of a Feather: Living On The Wind* and other books

****

"A commencement speech called 'This is Water' once addressed the fact that because goldfish spend their whole lives surrounded by water, they are oblivious to the fact that it even exists. They do not notice its wetness, its clarity, its movement, because they know nothing else. Similarly, we are often so caught up in our haphazard day-to-day lives that we do not recognize the important things that surround us. Have you ever listened to the way a bird calls? The way it changes its pitch so effortlessly? How one call is carried across the wind and returned as an echo seconds later?"

"Just one moment of awareness of the world around us can work wonders for the mind. Listen to the sound of tree leaves rustling, watch the way a bird ruffles his feathers, or notice the feeling of fresh air moving through your lungs on a crisp winter day. For those who live in cities, it is usually a park – or cemetery – that creates this connection. The beauty of Mount Auburn Cemetery invokes life and thought to anyone who visits. It may be the resting place of those who have passed, but it proves a stunning sanctuary of wildlife to those who are living."

"Surrounded by millions of people, Mount Auburn Cemetery is an oasis of greenery where so many attained the foundation of their knowledge and a passion for nature. In the everyday cycle of life here, Mount Auburn means different things to different people. Many of their intimate thoughts are passed along in this book. By reading these stories, you will understand part of its folklore and the impact this 'local patch' has had on so many."

– Richard Crossley / Crossley Books, author of the award-winning Crossley ID Guides and co-founder of Race 4 Birds, Pledge 2 Fledge, and Cape May Young Birders Club

****

"The superb writing of *Dead in Good Company* has moved me to try and visit Mount Auburn Cemetery as soon as possible and perhaps absorb some small fragment of the history of these birding pioneers (other than what the book has already presented). It's almost like trying to get insider information on some hot stock. I at first thought I would simply browse through the book but, instead, found it so riveting I couldn't put it down nor rush the reading. The work was done with such sensitivity, feeling and beauty of expression, by a group of distinguished writers."

– Sandy Komito, winner of The Big Year competition in 1998 and subject of the book, *The Big Year*, by Mark Obmascik, and the film of the same name, starring Owen Wilson (playing Sandy Komito), Jack Black and Steve Martin. Sandy Komito is author of his own account of The Big Year competition, *I Came, I Saw, I Counted*, and *Birding's Indiana Jones*

****

"I have long been a fan of John Harrison's photography, but the combination of stunning visuals and haunting essays detailing the rich history of Mount Auburn cemetery in *Dead in Good Company*, stories written by an eclectic selection of Massachusetts luminaries, makes it a must-read and gave me a new appreciation for wandering through the tombstones. Mount Auburn was the first rural cemetery in the country, and this is the first collection of photographs and stories about this final resting spot of poets and war heroes, Harvard professors and religious figures, that also captures the wonders of the wildlife that inhabit it."

– Michele McPhee, best-selling author, investigative reporter, radio talk show host

"More than a mere graveyard, Mount Auburn Cemetery is a haven for strollers – birdwatchers, historians, old folks, young students. That is what this book is: a quiet stroll through one of my hometown's hidden treasures, in the company of wonderful storytellers whose love for Mount Auburn shines through on every page. It is a place, and a book, to be visited again and again."

– William Landay, author of the New York Times bestseller, *Defending Jacob*

"*Dead in Good Company* is a treasure and a triumph! Great writing and absolutely breathtaking photography combined in a tribute to, of all things, a cemetery, but not just any cemetery. No matter how many times you've driven by Mount Auburn Cemetery in Cambridge, after reading *Dead in Good Company* you may soon find yourself pulling over and leaving your car to wander among the tombstones in search of the magnificent birds and other wildlife that inhabit 'Sweet Auburn.' Congratulations to all involved."

– Howie Carr, bestselling author of *The Brothers Bulger* and *Hitman*

"Having lived a life with wildlife, *Dead in Good Company* has touched me. Many people think wildlife is only in wild places they cannot visit. The problem is that in many instances we do not take the time to look right around us. This book is a jewel in bringing awareness to the reader that wildlife are our neighbors and live right around us if we would take the time to sit and watch. In our fast-paced life we often do not see what is right in front of us. Some of nature's masterpieces are available to everyone and what better place to teach our children the importance of conservation and the environment. These amazing essays should make everyone slow down and appreciate our wild neighbors. What our world needs is more of this type of book for the next generation to read."

– Walter C. Crawford, Jr., Founder and Executive Director, World Bird Sanctuary, Valley Park, MO

****

"A lively, fascinating collection of essays and stunning photographs that reveal the vibrancy and extraordinary beauty of the oldest landscaped cemetery in the nation. It may be a cemetery, but it teems with life, as *Dead in Good Company* shows so well. A wonderful book."

– Joseph Finder, *New York Times* bestselling author

****

"The good people who lie in Sweet Auburn are clearly double-dipping, as revealed in the fine essays and photos of *Dead in Good Company*. From its long history to the landscaping to those who now live here, and especially the birds, this special cemetery in the heart of Cambridge is truly heaven on earth."

– Donald Kroodsma, author of *The Singing Life of Birds*

Seeing the brilliant colors and patterns of warblers like this Blackburnian, set off against the subtle and delicate beauty of tree flowers, is something I look forward to every spring in New England. The dangling catkins of oak flowers attract insects, which attract hungry migrant warblers, and there is no place better than Mount Auburn Cemetery to experience this sublime expression of the season.

– David Sibley

Table of Contents

Acknowledgements xv

Foreword xvii

Preface xix

Alan Dershowitz, Introduction, *Life in Mount Auburn Cemetery* xxi

William Martin, *The Actor and the Hawk* 1

Hank Phillippi Ryan, *A Recipe for Memories* 6

Megan Marshall, *No Kin of Mine?* 11

Wayne R. Petersen, *The Yellow-rumped Warbler: An Old and Familiar Friend* .. 15

Phil Sorrentino, *Photo Essay* 26

Upton Bell, *Garden of Grand Illusion* 31

George Ellenbogen, *Mount Auburn Cemetery – Winter Icons* 34

Ray Flynn, *Voices Still Heard* 36

Dee Morris, *Looking for Some Inspiration* 41

Helen Hannon, *Where a Casual Conversation Can Lead* 44

Connie Biewald, *Life at Mount Auburn* 52

Sandy Selesky, *Photo Essay* 57

Linda Darman, *Walk With Me* 65

Dan Shaughnessy, *Hi Neighbor. Have a 'Gansett.* 70

Peter Filichia, *A Day With the Dean* 73

Eric Smith, *Photo Essay* 80

Gary Goshgarian, *Recollections Among the Dead* 84

Nathan Goshgarian, *Photo Essay* 88

Pierce Butler, *The Reality of Birds* 91

Mount Auburn Rarities, *Photo Essay by John Harrison* 97

Katherine Hall Page, *Sweet Auburn's Shades* 103

Jeff Meshach, *The Birds and the Trees* 108

Jim Renault, *Photo Essay* 112

Elsa Lichman, *Mount Auburn Dell February 22, 2013* 118

John Hadidian, *The Cemetery as Habitat and Home* 119

Nancy Esposito, *Birding In Mount Auburn Cemetery* 126

John Harrison, *Loving Lucy* 128

John Harrison, *Lucy* 133

John Harrison, *After Lucy* 135

Table of Contents

Peter Alden, *Mount Auburn or Bust*...139

David Pallin, *Photo Essay*..142

Leslie Wheeler, *Mount Aburn Cemetery: Three Beginnings and an Ending*..........145

Robert "Boz" Cogan, *Photo Essay*...149

Camilla H. Fox,
Connecting with Coyote in Mount Auburn Cemetery: Bonds that Last 154

Big Caesar and His Clan, *Photo Essay by John Harrison* 159

Big Caesar's Pups, *Photo Essay by John Harrison*...162

Ray Daniel, *The Lists of Mount Auburn*...167

Neil A. O'Hara, *Birds Among the Bodies*..170

Douglas E. Chickering, *Birds and Stones* 174

Clare Walker Leslie, *A Piece About Mount Auburn Cemetery, September, 2011*..177

Anneliese Merrigan, *Mount Auburn Sojourn*..180

Joe Martinez, *The Spotted Salamanders of Consecration Dell* 182

Shawn Carey, *Photo Essay* 186

Paul M. Roberts, *Preying in Mount Auburn: The Cemetery and Raptors*............194

Je Anne Strott-Branca, *Desert Jewels to Mount Auburn Jewels*..........................200

Gayle Lakin,
Mount Auburn Cemetery: A Tale Above and Below the Green Grass....................203

Kate Flora, *Dead in Good Company*..209

Ray Brown, *Lost in Sweet Auburn*...213

Wendy Drexler, *Heron at Willow Pond*...216

Andy Provost, *Photo Essay*...218

Kim Nagy, *The Owls*...223

Kim Nagy, *Photo Essay*...229

Maryanne O'Hara, *I Always Knew It Was Temporary*......................................239

Phil Ellin, *Photo Essay*..242

Sandra Lee, *Heaven's Playground*..247

Edith Maxwell, *My First Time* 252

Susan Moses, *Life Among the Dead: The Magic of Mount Auburn Cemetery*......254

Christopher Keane, *Under the Egyptian Gate* 261

Mary Pinard, *Direct Address* 266

Spring Migrants and Other Favorites, *Photo Essay by John Harrison*............268

Contributor Biographies 281

Acknowledgements

We wish to thank all of the authors, poets and photographers for both their contributions and their belief in our project. Their passion for "Sweet Auburn" is evident in every essay, every poem and every photograph, and their participation is a testament to the importance of Mount Auburn Cemetery.

The idea to write this tribute to Mount Auburn Cemetery has been years in the making. When we finally acted on our intention, our special contributors responded enthusiastically, magically appearing from all directions, helping to make our dream a reality. We are deeply indebted to you and we couldn't have done it without you!

Special thanks to Peter Filichia for his friendship and counsel for over five decades. Thanks also to Linda Konner of the Linda Konner Literary Agency for her advice and helpful observations throughout the *Dead in Good Company* adventure.

We are deeply grateful to our team that helped make it happen: Steve Gladstone was indispensable in organizing all our material and delivering a completed book. It wouldn't have been possible without him. Linda Darman played a critical role in preparing our manuscript for publication; thanks to Susan Moses for her generosity in assisting us with our project.

For their support always, we thank James Harrison, Mary Hogan, Corinne and Arthur Kinsman, Keith and Cathy Joyce, Tom Trevisani, Lorenzo Bolognese, Bob Chamberlin, Mike Fewell, Paul Harradine, Chief D. L. Fritz, videographer Ernie Sarro, Len and Sheila Lakin, Ruth MacDonald, John Amaral and Chaz and Virginia Brown. Also for their continued support, thanks to Joe and Karen Polvere, la famiglia Plati, Janet and Laura Aldorisio, Joel and all of the Prices, the Martochios, Dick and Cathy Minogue, Marybeth Lang, Kathleen Mahoney, Patricia Adams, our Days Hotel family and Virginia, Bob and Becky Parsons; Johnny, Lindsay and Oscar Kinsman; Bob and Edie Di Giorgio, Marion and Kathy Rolston, Pat Randall, David Gesner, and Marc Luca and the South Medford Brothers Deli Breakfast Club, and Bobbie and Frank Gatz. Also, Dick Haley, Bob Kelley, Bob Stymeist, Anna Piccolo, the Alewife hawkwatchers and the Menotomy Bird Club.

We wish to acknowledge the President of Mount Auburn Cemetery, David Barnett, and his dedicated staff for supporting our explorations over the years. Thank you Jennifer Johnston, Jessica Bussmann, Helen Abrams, Regina Harrison, Bree Harvey, Al Parker, Jimmy Hynes, Billy Shea and William Torres for your kindnesses through the years. Al and Jimmy, heartfelt thanks for so often leading us to the special birds and coyotes and foxes day after day, year after year.

Finally, our gratitude to the spirit of Mount Auburn. It led us around – or through – every obstacle and showed us how to get here.

- John Harrison and Kim Nagy

Foreword

When Jacob Bigelow and the rest of our founding fathers created Mount Auburn Cemetery in 1831, they envisioned a place that would serve the important functions of burial and commemoration of the dead while at the same time providing a beautiful, tranquil setting that would inspire the living. It was a brand new concept in this country, and it caught on. The success of Mount Auburn as a cemetery and its popularity as a tourist destination and beautiful landscape led to the Rural Cemetery movement and ultimately to the establishment of public parks like Central Park in New York and the Emerald Necklace in Boston. Today Mount Auburn is recognized as a National Historic Landmark because of its historic significance and influence on our country.

I often wonder if Jacob Bigelow and his colleagues could have possibly imagined how successful their visionary concept would be. Today, 184 years later, Mount Auburn attracts over 200,000 visitors per year, and they visit for many different reasons. Families and friends come to pay tribute to loved ones every day, and we continue to do about five hundred new burials per year. Others come to enjoy the beautiful landscape, the magnificent trees, the birds and other wildlife, or the amazing collection of funerary art and architecture. Many attend our educational programs and tours, and still others come to study history and learn about the notable residents of Mount Auburn. Some come to do all of the above.

The Board of Trustees and staff at Mount Auburn are currently developing a long-term strategic plan, and as part of that process we revisited our mission statement. It now states that:

Mount Auburn Cemetery:

- Inspires all who visit,

- Comforts the bereaved, and

- Commemorates the dead in a landscape of exceptional beauty.

It has been gratifying for me to read the collection of essays and enjoy the spectacular photographs in this book. It has confirmed to me that we are successfully carrying out our mission, and it has reminded me that the work every day of our dedicated staff to preserve and enhance the inspirational landscape that our founders envisioned and to continue to serve our clients and visitors with compassion and professionalism is extremely important and much appreciated. The stories and photographs collected here have particularly shown me that our efforts over the past twenty years to enhance the wildlife habitat value of Mount Auburn's landscape have been successful.

Thank you, John Harrison and Kim Nagy, for pulling this book together. It is nice to know we have so many good friends!

David Barnett
President and CEO
Mount Auburn Cemetery

Preface

It is inadequate to define Mount Auburn Cemetery in Cambridge, Massachusetts, as simply a final destination for the departed.

In essence, Mount Auburn Cemetery, or "Sweet Auburn" as it is sometimes called, is a place of life – an urban oasis set in sylvan tranquility. At every turn there are majestic trees from the four corners of the world, and on every path there are flowers of indescribable beauty. Mount Auburn Cemetery is, after all, America's first landscaped burial ground.

To the flocks of migrating birds that land, tired and hungry in the lush greenery each spring, it is a refuge for regeneration where they recover their strength, then take to the skies, gaining altitude and reaching the ancient flyways that take them north to raise their families. In the fall they repeat the journey in reverse, stopping at Mount Auburn Cemetery to refuel before they head to their winter home, hundreds if not thousands of miles away, to lands in the southern hemisphere.

In the waters of Halcyon Pond, Auburn Lake and Willow Pond live fish, frogs and other life that support the Great Blue Herons, Green Herons, other birds, foxes, coyotes and other wildlife that call Sweet Auburn home.

Every spring and fall, birders from all over New England, and even some from beyond our shores, celebrate this phenomenon of migration. Toddlers with small binoculars, accompanying their parents, are a regular sight at these times. Sweet Auburn gives them the gift of learning about the wonders of nature early in their lives. Every day in every season, photographers and wildlife enthusiasts comb the grounds, searching for the treasures that Mount Auburn Cemetery yields. The grounds teem with life no matter the weather or season; amazing events occur on the coldest day in January or on a beautiful spring day in May. There is life on every corner. That is the beauty of Mount Auburn Cemetery – a complete cycle of life, death, transformation and rebirth.

***

The authors, poets and photographers who have contributed to this work have come together to honor the wonder and affirm the life inherent in Mount Auburn Cemetery. They are a diverse group, and each of them tells a story of respect, love and honor for this special place.

This work is also an historical document. It is what we as early twenty-first-century individuals understand about this revered place, now. Perhaps the generation of Sweet Auburn walkers and watchers a hundred years from now will have access to this volume and they will be able to compare their thoughts and observations with ours. Will the same migrant birds – in the same numbers – descend on Sweet Auburn in May and September generations in the future? Will the occasional foxes and coyotes wander through here in search of food? Only time will tell.

Sweet Auburn. A cemetery, of course, but so much more.

Introduction

Life in Mount Auburn Cemetery

Mount Auburn Cemetery is a place where life meets death. It is alive with birds, squirrels, trees and other vibrant fauna and flora. These life forms exist comfortably alongside the dead, encroaching on their memorials and reminding visitors of the fleeting line between life and death.

For several years, I lived right near Mount Auburn Cemetery and walked its paths in search of solitude. This was a time before cell phones and so my frequent walks among the gravestones were disturbed only by the chirping of birds and the rustling of plants. I thought deep thoughts as I paused to read familiar names on tombstones. Occasionally I would come across the name of a person I knew in life. "Alas poor Yorich, I knew him..." The words of the bard always popped into my head on such occasions. Other times I came across famous names of those long gone and recalled the poetry of John Donne: "...never send to know for whom the bell tolls; it tolls for thee."

Everyone should spend some time experiencing the complex beauty of Mount Auburn Cemetery. Some go there only to bury their dead or to visit the graves of loved ones. That's a very different experience from walking its grounds and experiencing the interplay of life and death without focusing on a particular person. It produces different kinds of thoughts and different sorts of emotions.

There is a Jewish expression, *L'dor v'dor* which literally means "from generation to generation." I dedicated my most recent book to my own past and future generations, invoking those iconic words. I think I got the idea while walking through Mount Auburn Cemetery. It is not the only idea that came into my head while contemplating the passing of generations, the certainty of death and the vitality of life.

Thinking of the dead almost always includes self-referencing. When reading obituaries one is likely to compare the deceased with oneself in terms of age, illnesses and other factors. Similarly, a walk through a graveyard reminds us of our mortality. There but for the grace of God go I. When will it be my time? Make the most of one's remaining days. It can be both morbid and uplifting.

Life goes on punctuated by death. As Kafka once put it, "The meaning of life is that we all die." When Adam and Eve disobeyed God's commandment and ate from the Tree of Knowledge, the knowledge they received was of their own mortality. That Tree of Knowledge lives on among the gravestones in cemeteries like Mount Auburn.

Alan M. Dershowitz
Felix Frankfurter Professor of Law
Emeritus, Harvard Law School

William Martin

The Actor and the Hawk

You are going to meet the most famous actor – with the most infamous brother – of the nineteenth century. His name is Edwin Booth, and he sleeps on a gentle slope in the deep shade of a Norway maple. You are going to hear his story, because stories tell us our truths. Since the first storyteller sat at a campfire, stories have helped us to make sense of all that passes before us and of all that hides in the shadows beyond the firelight.

And this ancient cemetery is full of stories.

But as you approach Booth's grave, you notice a white Celtic cross. It marks the grave of someone less famous than Booth, but someone who managed to get himself a better spot, up there in the sunshine, up at the top of the slope.

And not only did he get a better spot. He got a guardian, too, a hawk who perches atop the cross and watches everything around him. The hawk causes you to stop, study, then slowly approach. He turns his eyes onto you and studies you right back and stays right where he is. You feel the intensity of his gaze and wonder, What's in it? Disdain? Curiosity? Or that mixture of disinterest and calculation that you see in the eyes of car salesmen, poker players, and doctors who don't bother with bedside manners.

The hawk is young, only recently fledged, so he does not yet realize that men are to be feared, even men with notebooks, cameras, and benign intentions. And he does not yet control the space around him with the authority that every raptor learns. The day will come when he will not offer you any expression at all, because he will not let you get close enough.

But now, you stand just ten feet from his perch. The words "Spes Unica" appear at the crux of the cross. "Our only hope." So the deceased was a good Christian…or at least a nominal one. But his name has been nearly obliterated by a century of rains, snows, and sun-soaked July mornings like this. There is a lesson here. But you are not learning it. You are more interested in the hawk.

He watches you a moment longer. Then he turns away. You conclude: disdain. The hawk thinks so little of you that you are worth no more of his time. Then, as you turn toward the grave of the actor, you realize that you have just given that hawk emotions, intellect, and qualities of perception he may not possess. You have anthropomorphized him. You have made him a character in the story you will tell of this day.

Stories are everywhere in Mount Auburn Cemetery, beneath every marker and atop every monument. Everyone who lies here lived as a character in his own drama. Some performed grand deeds. Others only dreamed them. But the moments they lived were as vivid, as colorful, as hot or cold, as joyous or terrifying, as any that we live now. That is why they have so much to teach us.

Edwin Booth was an avid supporter of Lincoln and a master interpreter of Shakespeare long before war divided the nation. On a night in 1864, he stood on a railroad platform, waiting to board a train. A young man stood in front of him, and when the train lurched, the young man slipped. Booth grabbed him by the collar and pulled him back. The young man that Booth saved from the crushing wheels of the train was Lincoln's son. But Booth could not save the young man's father a year later, or save his own brother from a mad act of vengeance. After that tragic Good Friday, Edwin Booth never spoke the name of Wilkes again. When he emerged from seclusion, he dedicated himself once more to the theater, to Shakespeare, to entertaining America from the stage.

Now a bronze bas-relief of the actor decorates his stone. Beneath it is a quote from the prophet Jeremiah: "I will turn their mourning into joy and will comfort them and make them rejoice from their sorrow." But you do not hear Jeremiah. You hear Genesis. You hear Abel hoping forever to expiate the sin of Cain. You hear a man who must have wondered for a quarter century, until his own death in 1891, if he could have done more as his brother's keeper. You hear one of the oldest human stories.

And there are so many others, in so many corners, telling their tales. They murmur to us in the rustling of the leaves and the sighing of the air itself.

In the mid-nineteenth century, a young Boston girl named Elizabeth Cary fell in love with a famous naturalist named Louis Agassiz. But he was married. And she was honorable. They did not marry until Agassiz's wife died. While he taught natural history to privileged young men at Harvard, she determined to teach young women. First came a school in her own house, then the "Harvard Annex," where Harvard professors taught young women for a fee, and finally Radcliffe College. In 1900, she was made its first president.

Edwin Land went to Harvard but never graduated. His head was too full of ideas to waste time on undergraduate courses. Instead, he invented instant photography, and in time everyone knew the meaning of "SX-70." Land did not live to see his company collapse when digital photography relegated instant cameras to the attic, along with buggy whips and butter churns. But he did live long enough to get an honorary degree from the school he quit.

Edward Everett, governor of Massachusetts, Congressman, college president, was considered the greatest orator of his time. In November of 1863, he went to Gettysburg to dedicate a cemetery. When he finished his speech, Abraham Lincoln said a few words, then sat and whispered to a friend, "They didn't like it. That speech won't scour." The next day, Everett wrote Lincoln a letter: "I should be glad if I could flatter myself that I came as near to the central idea of the occasion in two hours as you did in two minutes." Everett may also have been flattering Lincoln, but he knew. He knew that Lincoln's speech would "scour" forever. And of his own Gettysburg pronouncements, only that letter is remembered today.

The dead number near a hundred thousand on these 175 acres, beneath these 5,500 trees. You will never hear all their stories. You will never count all the trees. But you can see them all from a Godlike perspective. Climb the highest hill in the cemetery, atop which stands the magnificent Washington Tower. Climb the Tower to see the cemetery beneath you and all the hills of Eastern Massachusetts around you. On this July day, you will feel the summer wind booming down from Canada, giving the air a crisp, pellucid clarity found nowhere but New England. In such air, you believe that not only could you number every tree, but every leaf on every tree. Over there stands a copper beech, there a red oak, and there, the grandfather of New England trees…the sugar maple.

And out in the distance, at eye level with the top of the tower, the hawk and his siblings swoop and soar, testing their wings, feeling their nascent power, doing it all with the instinctive joy that Keats once heard in his nightingale. They ride on the breeze, oblivious to the dead, deaf to their stories, inured to their dramas and dreams.

It's as if they know that the past will never come again. But nature turns on a great cosmic wheel. And here, amidst the glades and groves and glorious vistas of Mount Auburn, the order of nature brings a comfort as profound as the purest faith ever imagined by rabbi, mullah, or Catholic priest. Agassiz and Land and Edwin Booth will not walk this way again. But others will come to bring invention, art, advancement. And in time, they too will return to earth. But the hawks will still hatch in the spring, and the leaves will flash silver and green in the summer breeze and fall soon after the first frost and bud again in the equinoctial light. That is the simplest message of Mount Auburn but the biggest story of all, the one about loss and renewal, death and rebirth.

So…it is time to go. You leave the Tower and walk down past Booth's grave again. You see a small headstone next to his wife's. You missed it earlier. It is the grave of their son, who died in childhood. The story of Booth's loss deepens, so too the story of his struggle to bring forth joy and renewal.

Then you glance again at the Celtic cross. The hawk has returned and perches once more in the sunlight. He gives you and Booth another disdainful look, then lifts his tail and lets go a long white squirt of guano. The grave marks the man. The hawk marks the grave.

It's as if the hawk is telling you, whatever superiority you may feel because you are enjoying a summer day on the right side of the grass, remember that you will soon join the famous old actor. So live well…and leave a good story for others to tell.

Red-tailed Hawk fledgling watched by William Martin on Sunday morning, July 2, 2014. Photo by John Harrison.

Hank Phillippi Ryan

A Recipe for Memories

You wouldn't think of "taste" in a cemetery. Senses initially awakened in Mount Auburn Cemetery do not include taste. Touch, certainly, the feel of the soft wind over your face. Sound, of course, the rustling sugar maple leaves and the persistent chirps of the crickets at twilight. And smell, too, the fragrance of cut grass and left-behind flowers. And sight, of course, the rolling hills and winding paths, the stately skyline of marble headstones, each with its etched-forever name and dates, bracketing the existence of a loved one.

Taste in a cemetery? Certainly Mount Auburn's lush scenery – and secluded green-bounded places of true privacy – has tempted many a canoodling couple to share wine and cheese and possibilities. But do not try it. It's tantalizing, but prohibited.

Still, taste – food – is part of Mount Auburn. Food, one of life's riches, and necessities, and one of the keys to our past. Madeleines or fried chicken, barbeque or popcorn or marshmallows over a campfire...when we think of memories, family memories especially, we can't help but think of food. An old family recipe is a precious legacy.

Growing up in Indiana, I remember – backyard cookouts and

the fragrance of Mom's chocolate chip cookies and the oregano-y scent of the homemade pizza and a coconut covered lamb-shaped cake she made on Easter and the spicy *haroses* on Passover. (We celebrated everything.)

She taught me how to make fried chicken and (as a grown-up New Year's Eve tradition) Oysters Rockefeller. We'd make popcorn in a special cast iron pot, and the family would share it watching Ed Sullivan on Sundays. Mom made a big production about the Thanksgiving turkey – even though later she admitted turkey was the easiest recipe in the world. There was also the great stuffing deception. She'd dramatically make two different bowls of stuffing, oyster and non-oyster, because we kids refused to eat oyster stuffing. Years later, many years later, I caught her in the kitchen on Thanksgiving, making one bowl of stuffing. And putting oysters in it. "Mom!" I stopped her, shocked. "You're putting oysters in the whole thing!"

"Yes, of course, dear," she said. "I've done that every year. You silly kids never knew."

Food in cemeteries? Sure. When I see Mom's headstone now, I think of the gooey chocolate chips and the crunchy popcorn, and not a Thanksgiving goes by that I don't tell the oyster dressing story. Food is our connection to the past, and recipes, handed down, become the physical link.

"Here's Mom's recipe book." My sister, mourning our loss, cried when she found it after Mom died. A Scotch-taped scrapbook of yellowing clips from newspapers and magazines, and even some handwritten instructions. I see her handwriting, with the precise dots over every "i" and the exact measurements of the ingredients for the chocolate chip cookies and the lamb cake and the goulash. It's all there. All in the familiar form, first listing the ingredients and quantities, then the numbered instructions.

"Read the whole recipe first," my mother would instruct, "or you'll never be able to cook it properly."

If you follow the recipe just right, my mother promised, you can't go wrong. It's chemistry. It's science. And to this day, her chocolate chip cookies come out the same every time.

It was not always so.

My Gramma Minnie, Dad's mother, made brunch for us every Sunday. After Sunday School, my cousin Larry and I would take the bus to 3140 North Meridian, and there Gramma Minnie and Grampa Dave would have laid out our brunch table. Gramma made tiny little pancakes covered with powdered sugar, and some sort of lemon sauce, and a fabulous, ridiculously delicious coffee cake with walnuts and chocolate. Made with real coffee. These days, they'd probably call it mocha-espresso walnut Bundt cake with crackled cinnamon glaze. But we just called it Gramma's coffee cake.

Gramma's coffee cake. Everyone asked her for the recipe. It was the family treasure hunt. The grail. But she would never do it. She would never tell. And she insisted there was no written recipe. "It's my secret," she would say. "You'll have to come to 3140 to get it." And we all did.

When Gramma died, the grandchildren chose from her silver and china and jewelry and her collection of Wedgewood shepherdesses. I got her watch, and her typewriter (one of those that came in a little suitcase, dear to me because she taught me to type). And in the midst of the estate articles, there it was in a little index card box. The grail. Gramma's recipe for coffee cake.

And it was incomprehensible. On a little three-by-five blue-lined index card, in Gramma's spidery handwriting. Oh, it was legible enough. But as a recipe? Impossible. We could read every word. But it didn't matter.

"Flour," it said. "Butter." And then: "Sugar." How much? No idea. And "coffee." Liquid coffee? Ground coffee beans? Instant coffee powder? How much? No idea. There were no quantities listed at all. She had left the legacy of the memory of that fabulous cake, but no way was she going to let us whip up the real thing.

Fannie Farmer would not have been pleased.

Food in cemeteries? Yes. Walk down Central Avenue in Mount Auburn – it's not a "green-lined" street, so you can park on the side. About halfway down, in the shade of a flowering dogwood, is the gravesite of Fannie Merritt Farmer.

"You'll have to move aside the ivy to see her full name," the guide told me. And indeed, her stone is simply a boulder, a mound of graceful granite tucked into a clearing in the grass, exactly the right size to be noticeable. Not at all grand, and almost demure.

Certainly there are more imposing memorials, fancier ones, more ostentatious. Fannie Farmer rests in the shadow of the William F. Harnden monument, the elaborate sculpture (including faithful dog) sculpted in memory of the man who developed the "express package delivery" system. And thank you, Mr. Harnden. We online shoppers are grateful.

But what Fannie Merritt Farmer accomplished is just as important.

She was a role model, and a groundbreaker in so many ways. During a time when marriage was expected, Fannie Farmer stayed single. What's more, she created not only a career, but a culinary system that stays with all of us who cook (and eat) even today.

If you are a person of a certain age, you probably still have a copy of her cookbook – and her debut as an author has changed the lives of families ever since it was printed (at her own expense!) in 1896 Boston.

"The mother of level measurements," they call her. She created the ground-breaking system that allowed one cook to duplicate, *exactly* duplicate, the work of another. She listed ingredients separately, with precise and standardized measurement. No more calling for "butter the size of an egg," says one story about her. No dollops or pinches or chunks or glops. No guessing or estimating or crossing fingers.

Fannie told middle-class housewives: "Correct measurements are absolutely necessary to insure the best results."

She goes on, in her seminal *Boston Cooking-School Cook Book*, to admit: "Good judgment, with experience, has taught some to measure by sight; but the majority need definite guides."

Can't you hear her oh-so-polite 1896 voice? It seems so obvious to us now, sharing a recipe, knowing it is reliable. Oh, we can tweak and change, but we still must understand the science that goes into making a delicious meal. "How much?" is every cook's resounding question. And "When?" And "How, exactly?" And "How does that work?" Fannie cooked up the reliable answers.

Fannie tells us, so patiently: "A cupful of liquid is all the cup will hold. A tea- or tablespoonful is all the spoon will hold."

And there were techniques: "To measure butter, lard, and other solid fats, pack solidly into cup or spoon, and level with a knife."

And when I saw this in Fannie's brownie recipe – "Mix ingredients in order given" – I burst out laughing.

My mother used to say that to me all the time. And that's the legacy, isn't it?

Thank you, Fannie. Thank you for Mom's chocolate chip cookies, and for allowing families everywhere to give their loved ones a legacy of deliciousness and memories and home and security. Thank you for giving us a way to recreate the tastes of childhood, no matter where we are.

Fannie, I wish my Gramma Minnie had listened to you. We have tried, and tried, and tried, but we still cannot reproduce that elusive coffee cake.

Megan Marshall

No Kin of Mine?

Although I have no ancestors or family members buried here, Mount Auburn Cemetery still serves as a lush garden of memories for me. Does it matter that none of them are my own?

The first monuments just beyond the gate bring vivid scenes to life. Spurzheim! Hardly anyone mourns Johann Gaspar Spurzheim today, or even recognizes the name, so prominent on his sarcophagus-like memorial. But, while researching Boston in the 1830s for my biography of the Peabody sisters, I learned that the great German phrenologist, who chanced to die on American soil, received one of the cemetery's first celebrity burials. Spurzheim, whose "science of mind" was based on the notion that character could be analyzed and improved by studying the shape of one's head, had been in Boston lecturing and giving consultations during the fall of 1832 when he contracted typhoid fever and died at the age of fifty-six. The Boston Medical Society issued a proclamation declaring "Dr. Spurzheim's decease . . . a calamity to mankind." His funeral procession began at Harvard's Medical College, paused at Boston's Old South Meeting House, where the Handel and Haydn Society sang a plaintive ode and eulogies were delivered in a packed sanctuary, then continued on to Cambridge with hundreds of mourners, many of them medical students, falling in behind.

Only paces farther along, I pass Nathaniel Bowditch's monument, with its seated statue by Robert Ball Hughes (America's first full-length figurative sculpture) showing off a gleaming bronze pate that would have impressed Spurzheim, who met Bowditch on his Boston tour. Here I think not of Boston and Cambridge, but of Salem. That's where the celebrated insurance mogul made his name as a mathematician and astronomer – and welcomed a child prodigy of learning, Elizabeth Palmer Peabody, to look through his telescope whenever she wished.

At age twenty-eight, by then leading a girls' school in Boston and serving as amanuensis for Rev. William Ellery Channing (d. 1842, Greenbriar Path), Elizabeth Peabody had been a member of Spurzheim's funeral parade. She and her sister Mary returned to Mount Auburn the following summer for recreation, as did so many Bostonians that first year and afterward. The sisters brought along their new friend, the politician Horace Mann, who managed to forget his sorrow over the recent death of his young wife Charlotte (buried in Providence) long enough to climb a tree and take in the view from one of Mount Auburn's hills. Perhaps this was the day Mary Peabody and Horace Mann fell in love, although it took ten years for Horace to propose.

On most visits to the cemetery, I walk directly along Central Avenue, take a right on Walnut, and veer off onto Orange Path to reach Pyrola, where I find the Fuller family plot. The showpiece is Margaret Fuller's cenotaph, erected in the mid-1850s, a few years after her tragic drowning, along with husband Giovanni Ossoli and son Angelino, in a shipwreck just three hundred yards offshore at Fire Island. All three are memorialized, and two-year-old Nino's remains are buried here. His parents' bodies were never found.

About halfway through the half-dozen years I spent researching and writing the life of Margaret Fuller – the great nineteenth-century intellectual and activist, whose epitaph rightly asserts her global influence – I moved to an apartment in Belmont within easy walking distance of Mount Auburn and this reminder of Fuller's historical significance. Although her childhood home on Cherry Street in Cambridge can be visited, few other landmarks survive, and I knew that Margaret Fuller, like the Peabody sisters and Horace Mann, enjoyed visiting the cemetery. Her close friend, the artist Sarah Clarke, produced a set of lithographs of "Sweet Auburn," perhaps around the time she illustrated Margaret's first book, *Summer on the Lakes, in 1843*, which recorded a journey they both took to Illinois, Wisconsin, and Michigan. Clarke's Mount Auburn lithographs, primarily landscapes depicting monuments, can be found in the collections of the Boston Athenaeum, which at one time also proudly held J.G. Spurzheim's brain.

While writing about Fuller I often walked over to the cemetery to pay my respects and commune imaginatively with my subject. Afterward I usually continued up Walnut Avenue to the summit of Mount Auburn and climbed Washington Tower to clear my head while admiring the views – changed since the days when Horace Mann ascended his tree, but no less refreshing. With Margaret's impressive but scarcely ostentatious cenotaph in mind, I scoffed at the massive twin obelisks that share the hilltop – absurd expressions of male vanity, I assumed – but never bothered to read their inscriptions. Until one day, over a year after my biography of Fuller was published. Could it be? The twin towers marked the graves of two of Margaret's uncles, Abraham and Henry Fuller! And Abraham's, the first to go up, had been installed before Washington Tower was built, making it the highest structure in the cemetery during the late 1840s – while Margaret was still alive and working as a foreign correspondent in Europe.

Abraham Fuller never married, he had no heirs, and he was one of the richest men in Cambridge when he died in 1847. He and his brother, I found out, had purchased Mount Auburn's Lot #1 when the cemetery was new, and then waited to memorialize themselves. Henry had a wife with whom to enjoy his fortune and who could join him in his half of the plot. I could only think solitary Abraham Fuller – who stingily refused Margaret a proper share of his wealth, money that would have allowed her to stay with her young family in Italy and might have prevented the tragic drownings – had written his own epitaph: "A merchant, enterprising, honest, successful; – satisfied with accumulation, – impelled in a manly desire of literary and intellectual pursuits; he became a member of the legal profession..."

Satisfied with accumulation. How much those few words said. I could picture Margaret's clashes with Uncle Abraham when he took over her family's finances after her father's early death and refused to fund expenses she considered necessary, from newspaper subscriptions to private school tuition for her younger sister. I could feel her sharp disappointment and bitter resignation when, a decade later, living on the brink of poverty in revolutionary Rome, she learned that Uncle Abraham had died and left her only $200 in his will. I imagined her chagrin if she'd lived to see his monument and consider the sum her uncle had committed to soaring vanity. My book was done, this history was over – but I was still angry on Margaret's behalf. Still mourning Margaret myself.

Wilson's Warbler. Photo by John Harrison.

Wayne R. Petersen

The Yellow-rumped Warbler: An Old and Familiar Friend

I honestly can't remember precisely when first I visited Mount Auburn Cemetery, though my handwritten childhood notes suggest it was May 10, 1959. That's the date when my mother first brought a kindred soul and me to the cemetery because we'd heard it was a fine place to see migrating birds during the month of May – especially warblers. In those halcyon days of my youth, virtually every outing produced new birds for my rapidly expanding life list, and every new encounter whetted my appetite to find others. Despite the fact that on one of my daily pedestrian commutes to elementary school I had previously added the "Myrtle" Warbler to my list, I was dazzled by the abundance of this familiar species at Mount Auburn on that glorious day in May more than a half century ago. I especially appreciated the species' rather sluggish behavior that made its distinctive yellow rump and dashes of yellow at the sides of its breast and on its crown easy to observe.

Yellow-rumped Warbler. Photo by Kim Nagy.

Yellow-rumped Warbler. Photo by Kim Nagy.

Yellow-rumped Warbler. Photo by Kim Nagy.

I have no idea how many times I've visited Mount Auburn Cemetery since then, but regardless of the number, the "Myrtle" Warbler has often been a constant. Whether it be spring or fall, the likelihood of encountering this generally common and widespread species somewhere in the cemetery is often high. Its distinctive and frequently-uttered *check* note alerts me to its presence, and in the spring its rather colorless *seet-seet-seet-seet-seet* (slightly higher in the middle) song usually gives away its whereabouts. But let me digress. A perusal of current field guides scarcely mentions this ubiquitous species. The reason is that the "Myrtle" Warbler now bears the name Yellow-rumped Warbler. Once thought to be a distinct species, the "Myrtle" Warbler and its western counterpart, the "Audubon's" Warbler, were determined in the 1970s to be one and the same species masquerading as two, so they were taxonomically "lumped." Today both forms are called Yellow-rumped Warbler and bear the scientific name *Setophaga coronate*, which, literally translated, means "crowned moth-eater."

With the arrival of the first mellow morning in mid-April I expect to find dozens of Yellow-rumps leisurely sallying after flying insects along Indian Ridge, or quietly foraging with Ruby-crowned Kinglets and Palm Warblers at eye level in the shrubbery. Early in the season before the caterpillars emerge and the oaks begin to flower is the best time in the cemetery to fully appreciate handsome male Yellow-rumps with their blue-gray backs, black masks, upside down black U on their breasts, and white corners to their tails. As caterpillars begin their emergence in early May, Yellow-rumps tend to forage higher in the canopy, thus rendering their distinctive colors and markings less obvious, except of course their telltale yellow rumps.

Ruby-crowned Kinglet. Photo by John Harrison.

Palm Warbler. Photo by John Harrison.

Where do these harbingers of the great spring migration soon to follow come from and where are they headed? Many Yellow-rumps spend the winter in coastal thickets along the Atlantic seaboard from Cape Cod to Florida, sustained by nutritious berries capable of serving as substitutes for their preferred protein-rich arthropod diet during the warmer months. Others may have overwintered in the Caribbean or Mexico enjoying the balmy climate of the subtropics. As winter relinquishes its grip on New England, however, the first male Yellow-rumps of spring slowly begin their northward journey to breeding grounds located primarily in the great boreal forests of Canada. Quite possibly a Yellow-rumped Warbler seen foraging in the Dell at Mount Auburn in mid-May could end up in northern Labrador or the James Bay region of Ontario two weeks later. By late May female Yellow-rumps will have joined the males on the breeding grounds.

It is interesting to consider not only where the Yellow-rumps and other warbler species at Mount Auburn Cemetery come from, but also how they get there. Like most small songbirds, Yellow-rumped Warblers migrate at night, sometimes hundreds of miles in a single evening. Shortly after dark on clear nights with winds from the southwest and rising temperatures, sometimes hundreds or even thousands of tiny migrants take to the air bound for breeding grounds many miles away to the north. Point of origin, local flying conditions, and flight speed determine how far a migrant may fly on a particular night, and the distance may vary from under two hundred to up to six hundred miles, especially for species making non-stop flights from the Yucatan Peninsula across the Gulf of Mexico to the Gulf Coast of the United States. Because of where they spend the winter, most Yellow-rumps are unlikely to regularly make such lengthy, non-stop flights. Navigating at night is another matter. Migration studies conducted in planetariums have demonstrated that celestial navigation is important for many species. When polar stars are obscured, birds have difficulty orienting themselves correctly. This is why rainy or foggy evenings in Cambridge are frequently followed by especially large numbers of migrants at Mount Auburn the next morning. Many disoriented nocturnal migrants put down in the cemetery rather than continue traveling under adverse flight conditions. Well-planted, food-rich oases like Mount Auburn Cemetery provide welcome refuge for such grounded migrants until flight conditions improve. Often these migrants will spend several days in the cemetery resting, feeding, and preparing themselves for the next leg of their migration.

It's fascinating to watch warblers foraging in the cemetery. A watchful eye will detect subtle differences. Yellow-rumped Warblers seem to spend a lot of energy sallying after insects (remember "moth-eater") at mid-level in trees, often from the outer ends of branches. At the same time Wilson's and Canada Warblers actively perform aerial pirouettes as they pursue winged prey in the low-growing laurels and rhododendrons on the slope overlooking Mary Baker Eddy Pond. Ovenbirds and Northern Waterthrushes walk stealthily beneath dense shrubbery in search of terrestrial invertebrates, Black-and-white Warblers creep like striped nuthatches around the trunks and limbs of large trees, and the much sought-after Cape May and Blackburnian Warblers inconspicuously seek tiny insects or sip nectar from the highest oaks and conifers in the Dell. These variable foraging behaviors offer a clue as to how the thirty or so regularly occurring warbler species that annually visit Mount Auburn Cemetery help to reduce competition between species. Imagine if everyone visiting an ice cream parlor ordered the same kind of ice cream!

Ovenbird. Photo by John Harrison.

Northern Waterthrush. Photo by John Harrison.

Black-and-white Warbler. Photo by John Harrison.

Blackburnian Warbler. Photo by John Harrison.

Cape May Warbler. Photo by John Harrison.

While it's true that most Yellow-rumped Warblers stopping at Mount Auburn in the spring continue on to points north to breed, this familiar species also nests in Massachusetts. The majority of the Commonwealth's breeding population nests from late May to late July in the higher hills of Worcester County and westward. Here they prefer areas where spruce, hemlock, or white pine predominate; they are often most common at the edges of such forests. For those familiar only with the rather insipid migration song of the Yellow-rumped Warbler, on its breeding grounds it sings a more forceful rendition that often resembles that of a Dark-eyed Junco, a species often found sharing its habitat. The nest of the Yellow-rump, a cryptic structure I've only personally twice successfully located, may be placed from four to fifty feet off the ground, usually in a conifer and located on a branch away from the trunk. The lining of a Yellow-rump's nest is interesting in that it typically includes small feathers which tend to partially conceal the eggs when the adult warbler is away from the nest. Four to five buff-colored, speckled eggs hatch in about twelve days, and by mid-August most juvenile Yellow-rumps have fledged and begun to flock with other forest species prior to initiating fall migration. During this late summer season often the most distinctive field mark of the juveniles is their yellow rump, the rest of their brownish plumage heavily streaked and quite unlike the handsome gray and white feathering of their parents.

By mid-September Yellow-rumped Warblers are on the move. Though they are seldom as numerous at Mount Auburn at this time of year as during the spring, they can nonetheless be found by the patient observer willing to look through resident flocks of chickadees, nuthatches, and Downy Woodpeckers with which they often associate, along with other warbler species, most notably Blackpolls. Their distinctive and oft-given *check*-note is a good indicator of their presence at this time of year. In fall the upperparts of most Yellow-rumps are brownish in color, and even the adult males wear a plumage less strikingly blue-gray than in the spring. Their eponymous yellow rump, however, is still obvious.

When September rolls into October and the colored leaves of autumn begin to fall, the numbers of migrant Yellow-rumps increase (sometimes reaching lavish abundance), especially in berry-rich thickets along the coast. There they harvest the fat-rich fruits of shrubs like bayberry, cedar, buckthorn, Virginia creeper, viburnum, and even poison ivy. It is their ability to harvest and successfully digest these abundant fruits and berries that allows many Yellow-rumps to successfully remain in Massachusetts throughout the winter, thus making the species virtually a permanent resident in the Bay State. Winter numbers are highly variable, however, and are largely determined by the magnitude of the late fall bayberry crop. Noted Cambridge ornithologist, William Brewster, even recorded seeing a few Yellow-rumped Warblers in the Cambridge region in mid-winter (*Birds of the Cambridge Region*, 1906).

My personal experiences with Yellow-rumped Warblers have run full circle, from initial encounters as a youth growing up in Wellesley when the species was still called "Myrtle" Warbler, to its present-day classification as Yellow-rumped Warbler. I have found their nests, banded them, observed them at the extreme limit of their range in northern Alaska, documented the "Audubon's" form in Massachusetts, witnessed thousands of them during autumn migration "fallouts," tallied dozens on Christmas Bird Counts, had them come aboard ships miles from shore, and watched them feeding in courtyards in Cuba. Wherever I see them, Yellow-rumps register a sense of familiarity, like meeting an old friend. But especially heartwarming is encountering them at Mount Auburn every spring, when they invariably bring to mind those first youthful encounters in the cemetery so many years ago.

Catbird. Photo by Kim Nagy.

Phil Sorrentino

Black-and-white Warbler

Common Yellowthroat

Indigo Bunting

Great Horned Owl

Magnolia Warbler

Northern Parula

Ovenbird

Scarlet Tanager

Upton Bell

Garden of Grand Illusion

I fled Him, down the nights and down the days,
I fled Him, down the arches of the years;
I fled Him, down the labyrinthine ways
Of my own mind; and in the mist of tears
I hid from Him, and under running laughter.
— Francis Thompson

It is not the Garden of Eden.

It is not the Garden of Good and Evil.

It is not the Garden of the Finzi Contini's.

You don't have to cross the River Styx to enter it.

You just have to cross Mount Auburn Street and suspend disbelief before you enter the Holy of Holies. The mind must be willing to take a trip that equals or betters Alice's journey at the end of the rabbit hole.

There, on a day in early autumn, I begin my trip. I have come many times to this New England version of the Wailing Wall. The leaves are turning and my life is too. No Jane Fonda workout is going to save me from my final destiny.

As I cross this threshold of the living and dead souls, I am struck by the beauty of this place with its meandering paths of flowers and towering trees inhabited by birds of all feathers. I hear the wind whistle around me. I hear the birds communicate with each other. They are the sentinels that both watch and lead me. I hear the sounds of the living and the voices of the dead. Graveyards are the noisiest places on earth. I see people standing, sitting and kneeling before their beloved ones. They come to laugh and cry and communicate their memories and recriminations.

On this day, I seek the high ground where the great tower hovers over the land. At one time, it was the highest point in Cambridge. It is a place of beauty as well as a place of awe. It looks down on the mighty Charles River where Native Americans once paddled their canoes. From the top of the tower, you can see the city on the hill, Boston, in all its glory. You can see in all directions, Mount Wachusett some fifty miles away, the local countryside and the hills of Central Massachusetts.

I take my time as I walk the many paths that are lined with great monuments and the small stones that herald lives well lived. My mind wanders back to my parents, Bert and Frances. They were Tracy and Hepburn to me, fascinating to me, but they died when I was too young. They should be buried here where I could visit them in this mystical garden. I reflect on them and myself as I continue toward the tower. My life is now at a point where the soul is more important than the body. I remember Bert and Frances who brought me into life, kicking, screaming and fearful into the first dawn's early light. They imbued me with joy and laughter and a sense of the extraordinary. They were loving and caring, unpredictable and somewhat eccentric. Like this Garden, they were celestial in their own right. Their time on earth was short, like the seasons.

From the birth of spring flowers to the death of fall foliage, life is short for all of us and nothing reflects this more than the Garden.

The structure appears through the trees and very shortly I will arrive at the New England Tower of Babel. As I continue to climb, my mind is racing and my heartbeat grows faster. I reach the front of the tower and have only to climb that circular stairway to the top. There are many people this day going up and down at their own pace. I was hoping to be alone at the top with only the view and my thoughts, but this was not possible.

As I climb the steps that represent the stages of my life, I think of this as the long goodbye, the end of a dream. I emerge from the long winding stairway to bright sunshine and a lot of voices, many in foreign tongues but, after all, this is the Tower of Babel. I look out on a blazing array of color. It is fall foliage and the Garden is alive in all its glory. I feel like a modern day Ulysses roaming the world, a moveable feast filled with dreams of success, mitigated by failure. My walk through this special place has given me a final perspective on life, death and infinity. I wait for the crowd to leave. Alone with my thoughts, I am grateful for another day. The sun is going down now and I must leave.

Suddenly I feel cold. When I reach the bottom step, I turn my back on the tower and all it represents. I do not hide my tears. There is no warm wind of spring this time to absolve me. I know the gates to this magical Garden will be closing soon but I'm in no hurry to leave. I will reach the gates in my own time and if they are closed, I will do what I always do in life, I will climb them.

Ozymandias

I met a traveler from an antique land
Who said: Two vast and trunkless legs of stone
Stand in the desert. Near them on the sand,
Half sunk, a shatter'd visage lies, whose frown
And wrinkled lip and sneer of cold command
Tell that its sculptor well those passions read
Which yet survive, stamp'd on these lifeless things,
The hand that mock'd them and the heart that fed.
And on the pedestal these words appear:
"My name is Ozymandias, king of kings:
Look on my works, ye Mighty, and despair!"
Nothing beside remains: round the decay
Of that colossal wreck, boundless and bare,
The lone and level sands stretch far away.

— Percy Bysshe Shelley

33

George Ellenbogen

Mount Auburn Cemetery – Winter Icons

For John Harrison, bird photographer

Icicles from the elbows
Of ash and elm declare
the trees are pondering winter
silence. Their tenants,
sparrows and finches, syllables
of December, range
on these boughs
 and remain.

Warblers and buntings have taken
melody and plumage to other places,
pools with warmer splashes
and shelter of leaves, leaving
only memories of trysts
with darker seasons.

We plan annual squints each May
for first flashes of yellow, indigo,

                                    and melody

that flutes out promises of green,
flourishes of bunting,
but finger icons that return us
to snow coated boughs, photos
of colder twilights, fewer birds, fewer
watchers and spreads of oak and ash
with finches and sparrows
in this season of ice
chirping against darkness.

Ray Flynn

Voices Still Heard

Often times while driving by Mount Auburn Cemetery in Cambridge, I'm compelled to pull the car over and visit one of America's most beautiful treasures. Its majestic beauty is only exceeded by its simplicity and tranquility. If you want to connect to the beauty of nature and America, Mount Auburn Cemetery is the place to visit; but if you want to reflect on America's and Massachusetts' rich political and literary heritage, Mount Auburn Cemetery is also the place to visit. But first let me tell you a little about my lifetime love affair with cemeteries.

One of the things I often did during my weekends off when I was U.S. Ambassador to the Vatican was to visit cemeteries throughout Italy and other parts of Europe, including Normandy, and even Northern Africa. I would read the history of famous battles and visit the graves and study the headstones of the fallen U.S. and British war heroes. Sometimes my brother Dennis and I would even be waiting for the U.S. Military Cemetery gates to open in the early morning. We would also be some of the last ones to leave in the early evening. Dennis was a decorated Vietnam veteran and a student of military history and had an enormous respect for those who lost their lives in service to our country. When he visited me in Rome, we would go to a local veterans' club and hang out with the military veterans who might also be there visiting the battleground cemeteries. It was a remarkable and moving experience listening to all the stories from the combat veterans. I'd talked to U.S. Senators, Governors, authors and even Pope John Paul II at the Polish Cemetery at Monte Cassino near Naples, the resting place for members of the Polish Resistance who fought the Nazis at the end of World War II. But where did my interest in visiting cemeteries all begin? As a little boy growing up in Boston.

Whether it was taking the streetcar to Calvary Cemetery, Mount Hope, Cedar Grove or Mount Auburn in Cambridge, each year, usually on Memorial Day and July 4th, my mother, aunt, three brothers, and I would head out on our daylong journey. We had no car in those days, so we took the Boston Elevated and did a lot of walking. We often met scholars and historians who were anxious to inform people about the history and told some stories about who was buried there. Not just the famous, but some of the more ordinary ones as well. But they were all interesting.

Years later, while I was Mayor of Boston and attending a close friend's funeral in Cambridge, my wife Kathy and two of our children and I toured Mount Auburn Cemetery. I told them how we often visited this burial ground when I was a kid. I still remember seeing the gravestones of some of the famous Boston mayors like Josiah Quincy and Harrison Gray Otis and Massachusetts governors like Edward Everett, Roger Wolcott and William Russell. Many poets like Henry Wadsworth Longfellow and Amy Lowell. But I also took my kids over to the gravesite of U.S. Senator Henry Cabot Lodge, Jr., who came from a very prominent Massachusetts Republican family. Lodge fought in World War II, and during his long distinguished political career was U.S. Ambassador and U.S. Senator, defeating Governor James Michael Curley in 1936 in a partisan and heatedly debated election. He later lost his Senate seat to Congressman John F. Kennedy in 1952.

But at his gravesite that day, I shared a private story that I had never told before about U.S. Ambassador to Vietnam Henry Cabot Lodge, Jr. I said when I was elected to the Massachusetts

House of Representatives in 1970, a suitable memorial had never been erected in Boston to the legendary Mayor James Michael Curley. The reason was probably a combination of Yankee Brahmin bias against Irish Catholics and typical political jealousy, which is a trademark of Boston politics. No mayor succeeding Curley wanted to honor him. Maybe they were afraid that *The Boston Globe* would criticize them because of Curley's past. But I was an admirer of "Curley, the Mayor of the Poor." He was a fighter for the downtrodden and needy. He advocated social and economic justice policies that were not at all popular with the downtown establishment.

One of the early bills I filed in the Massachusetts House of Representatives was to create a Select Blue Ribbon Commission to recommend a memorial for Curley. Still there was wide political opposition. I was selected to be Chairman of the Commission. The first call I made was to former U.S. Senator Henry Cabot Lodge, Jr., Curley's perceived bitter political rival. I knew that Lodge would attract the wide media attention that was needed to turn things around for Curley. Curley top aide and later judge Dan Gillen cautioned me against inviting Lodge to testify. "They never liked each other," he told me. Out of the blue, I called Senator Lodge who invited me up to his home on the North Shore. We talked for a couple of hours and he agreed that he would come to the State House for the public hearing. The hearing room was crowded with scholars, historians, college students, elected officials, media and political junkies. If some people had expected that Lodge would tell unflattering stories about Mayor Curley, they were in for a big surprise. The former Republican Vice Presidential candidate moved the room to tears with his eloquence and sincere respect for Curley. I remember Dick Flavin of WBZ-TV saying that not only did Lodge steal the show, but he gave the beloved Curley a tribute that nobody expected. Lodge became very melancholy when talking about his one-time rival. He convinced the Commission that Curley was indeed worthy of the honor of having a statue erected across the street from historic Faneuil Hall in downtown Boston.

By the time I finished telling that story about Lodge and Curley at the grave of Ambassador Lodge, over twenty people had joined us to listen in. One history buff and Harvard professor said to me, "Mayor, that's a great story; I never heard that before. Honor between rivals, I guess." "Sounded like they privately respected each other, but didn't want the public to know it," I said.

Recently, I was talking to Gerard Coyne, the owner of Coyne's Pub in Tullycross, County Galway, Ireland. Gerard is a cousin to Mayor James Michael Curley. He was recalling the day that I visited my wife's uncle John Coyne in Gerard's pub, then called Curley's Pub and owned by Mayor Curley's uncle. I was with a couple of Massachusetts State Legislators, Jim Hart of Dorchester and Maurice Donahue of Holoyke. We talked for hours about Mayor Curley's family from Oughterard, County Galway, Ireland.

The last thing Gerard Coyne said to me was, "I'd love to have a photo hanging in my pub of the three Boston Mayors whose families came from Connemara. That's incredible; no other city in America could make that claim." In my opinion, public service, being well educated, all without thought of personal financial gain has been the hallmark of Irish politicians in America. "Mayor Curley, Mayor Flynn, whose grandparents were from Spiddal, and our present Mayor Martin Walsh, whose parents are from Rosmuck and Carna. That's quite an honor," Coyne said. Well, no such photo exists, but I'm sure one exists of the Rascal King (Curley) and Mr. Pure Blue Blood (Lodge). Yes, we said a prayer at the Mount Auburn grave of Ambassador Henry Cabot Lodge. But we also were reminded about a political era in America when rivals had respect for each other, but more importantly, could work together for the "common good." Both men were confident of their own ability and intelligence and didn't need to undermine one another. Politicians were committed to the unity and the building of our country, not exploiting party differences. Yes, you can learn a lot about life in a cemetery.

The Irish and Yankee politicians in America did more to make our country great going back to Roosevelt, Kennedy, and Reagan. They may have come over in different ships and from different countries, but nobody can argue that they fought for what they believed and worked hard for themselves and our country.

Curley and Lodge seem like a political anomaly, but there is no doubt they were experienced, knew how to get the job done and made America stronger.

So if you want to see the beauty of America and listen to the voices of some of the people who made our state and nation great, stop by Mount Auburn Cemetery in Cambridge. It's the best ticket in town.

Morning in the Dell. Photo by Kim Nagy.

Dee Morris

Looking for Some Inspiration

The massive gate at the entrance to the cemetery sets the mood. Designed as a re-creation of a style popular in ancient Egypt, it guards a spectacular landscape adorned with elegant monuments. This sacred space is also dedicated to the life stories of the famous as well as the narratives belonging to all the people who rest within its perimeters. Mount Auburn is timeless yet always changing.

The living come here for many reasons. My first visit, way back in the 1980s, was part of a group effort to save an endangered community garden. The Victorian owner of the site where we grew our cucumbers and marigolds was Charles Mason Hovey (1810-1887), an iconic Cantabrigian. Throughout his long lifetime, he had embraced anything to do with American horticulture, including the development of Mount Auburn. He was an enthusiastic member of the Massachusetts Horticultural Society from its very beginning. I had learned that Hovey and his family were buried on Mound Avenue at the corner of Spruce. This was my pilgrimage. I needed the inspiration.

Hovey's story had already enriched me. As a self-made man of seemingly boundless energy, he grew up in Cambridge's Central Square where he became interested in raising new, hardier strains of fruit, especially strawberries. Charles went on to edit *The Magazine of Horticulture,* an early clearinghouse of useful information, in addition to publishing *The Fruits of America,* a several-volume set illustrating native varieties in all their abundance. Of immediate interest to me was the fact that the community garden site had been a very small portion of his forty-acre nursery in mid-Cambridge. We were harvesting tomatoes where he had planted multiple varieties of pears, apples and peaches that flourished in the Boston climate. It seemed prophetic to read his views on open space: "What the busy people of the city need is pure air, the sight of green trees…extensive grounds, where they can enjoy the pleasures of the country." In spite of the odds, we were hoping to have our garden preserved as a living testimonial to an optimist's unquenchable passion for growing useful and beautiful plants.

My Mount Auburn search did not end the way I had anticipated. The corner lot on Mound Avenue was a level, spacious area close by some ornately beautiful memorials owned by well-to-do Bostonians. Mature trees formed a neighborly backdrop. On the Hovey site, however, there was no marker to commemorate Charles, his wife or any other member of his immediate circle. This was beyond the unexpected. I left the cemetery feeling that I had been cheated out of reading an inscription, enjoying a symbolic fruit design…something…anything. Inspiration was at a standstill.

Then everything moved forward. Over the course of time, not surprisingly, we lost our campaign to keep the garden. When it was paved, there were a few day lilies that made a cameo appearance near the sidewalk. I sought out the quiet of Mount Auburn. At first I followed the sinuous paths randomly, then curiosity got the better of me. Where were the other members of the Hovey family buried? What were they like? I began compiling notebooks. First, I started with Cambridge horticultural news then found tidbits such as the comment that Mr. and Mrs. Hovey enjoyed hosting strawberry festivals at their home for the entire neighborhood. By reading his seed and plant catalogs, I realized that Charles named his prize-winning camellias after people he loved. One favorite was called the "Charles H. Hovey," a jaunty blossom that honored a son who became a florist. I marked up copies of the Mount Auburn map and documented the Hovey locations. Every visit, month after month, ended with a courtesy call at the unmarked grave site on the corner of Mound Avenue. A thought kept recurring – there must be hundreds of stories in this eternal city.

In 1986 the cemetery established the Friends of Mount Auburn. Their mission is to promote a greater understanding and appreciation of the many natural and historical resources of this carefully considered landscape. I joined and was asked to present one of the first programs. The topic, naturally, was C.M. Hovey and all his contributions.

Other stories have continued to emerge. I am a fan of Moses Pond (Trefoil Path) who was a Cambridgeport blacksmith and a frequent contributor to Hovey's *Magazine of Horticulture*. Charles told him that his opinion counted, especially because Pond knew how to revitalize clay soil. On a different social level, Abby Adams Angier, a niece of John Quincy Adams, is memorialized by a Gothic Revival monument located on Yarrow Path. I think of it as a beautiful marble valentine set there by her husband, John. Abby's love for this Medford, Massachusetts, schoolmaster gave her the courage to pursue happiness. There are so many more connections, revelations about the human personality and opportunities to make sense out of what is going on in my own life. When I lead a tour, I hope that others will develop their own insights. It is impossible for me to go to Mount Auburn without spending some quality time looking at the empty space on Mound Avenue. I need the inspiration.

Helen Hannon

Where a Casual Conversation Can Lead

It was the American Civil War that brought me to Mount Auburn Cemetery. A conversation with a friend led to my first visit there. He was a longtime member of the Fifth Massachusetts Volunteer Battery re-enacting unit. Somehow Mount Auburn Cemetery had come up and he mentioned that Nathan Appleton, a member of the Fifth Mass during the Civil War was buried there. Appleton, along with Henry D. Scott, John F. Murray, Thomas E. Chase, and George L. Newton, members of the actual Fifth Massachusetts regiment, had written *History of the Fifth Massachusetts Battery* published in 1902. My friend had always been meaning to visit Appleton's grave, but just hadn't gotten around to it. Not long after that, I was driving past Mount Auburn and decided to stop in and ask about Appleton's grave.

The time was about 9:00 A.M. and it was a very cold morning. The people in the office looked in their files and gave me the location of the Appleton lot. As we were doing this, a woman walked by and asked in a friendly way about Nathan Appleton. Why was I interested in his grave? I explained that I was asking for a friend. This was my introduction to Janet Heywood. In addition to Mount Auburn's unique aura, it was Janet who was one of the big draws for me. At the time, she said that meeting people in the office was how she learned more history about Mount Auburn. Meeting Janet turned out to be a good way for me to be introduced to the unique history of the cemetery. Through her, I discovered their lectures, programs, etc. That early morning visit began my long connection with the world of Mount Auburn. Since then, I got to know other staff members and program presenters who made my attachment with Mount Auburn grow deeper and deeper.

On a Memorial Day, possibly the very next Memorial Day after meeting Janet, the Fifth Mass came over to Mount Auburn for a ceremony at Appleton's grave. After participating in Cambridge's Memorial Day parade, they came in their open truck, in full uniform, and marched to the site where they had a brief memorial service. My part was to go ahead by about five hundred feet to lead them down the correct roads. The Appleton family plot has a striking monument, and the service was brief and gracefully simple. These small, but moving, events are one of the reasons why people join re-enacting units. It presents the opportunity to participate in history in a way that has a special meaning. My friends and I attended other Mount Auburn events – Longfellow's birthday, walking tours – and I have done research there. The conversation with my friend and then Janet opened up a very special place for all of us.

It was not a direct route that led me to my interest in the Civil War. The first step began when I started collecting nineteenth-century vintage clothing. Then I was told about a local dance group, the Commonwealth Vintage Dancers, who did nineteenth- and early twentieth-century dance events. They accurately researched ballroom dances, and both the dance group members and the participants wear the proper clothing for whatever era is being featured. Then along came a totally unexpected event that influenced many, many people. The Ken Burns documentary, *The Civil War*, aired for the first time. I believe it was this series more than anything else that brought new people to Civil War history. That program held the country spellbound for five days. There has always been a strong contingent studying the Civil War, either as professional or amateur historians. However, this series introduced many more people, including myself, to a very significant time in the history of the United States.

My path seriously began when I met Civil War re-enactors at the vintage dances and at various organizations. I went to a few local Civil War events. In the early days of the 1990s, they were very small, often with people who had been doing re-enacting since the Centennial in the 1960s. I decided to read an overview of the war years and chose James McPherson's *Battle Cry of Freedom*. My thinking was that it would be interesting and would give me basic information about the era and that would be that. The unexpected result was that I began reading more books, then even more. Now I have read many, many books about the Civil War. My particular interest is Massachusetts in the Civil War.

Studying the Civil War is somewhat addictive. No matter what your interests may be – military or civilian – there is a wide spectrum from which to choose. Part of the reason why this war attracts so many people and has been studied so extensively is because there are so many areas in which to specialize. It was a huge cataclysm in United States history. It is almost too big to understand fully. The Centennial in the 1960s started the practice of re-enacting locally up North, but it exploded in the 1990s. After the Ken Burns program, it went from sparsely attended re-enacting events to having hundreds show up, portraying soldiers and civilians.

People getting together at re-enactments was not unlike other groups that come together at Mount Auburn, such as bird-watchers, historians, horticulturalists, etc. There are many tour leaders who have spent hours walking around Mount Auburn and researching the sculptures, horticulture, wildlife and the stories of the people who now rest there. They love to share their information. I no longer do much re-enacting. In fact, the numbers of people re-enacting around here has dwindled considerably from the mid-1990s. However, that has not stopped my interest in the Civil War.

Older cemeteries offer an insight into the effect the war had on generations. Walking through Mount Auburn there are countless reminders. Some are monumental tributes, like the *Colossal Sphinx* acknowledging the end of African-American slavery. Others are small gravestones that include the name of the battle where the soldier died. Sometimes the fallen are honored with a cenotaph memorial because their bodies were never found. It was important to have a place for the families to symbolically honor their lost relatives. There are gravestones of men who lived to a significant old age, but arrangements were made to include their regiments on the stone at their death. Oftentimes, these former soldiers had died decades after the war and from old age, and not necessarily from wounds or sickness acquired during their service. This was the impact of the war on their lives. It created a bond and experience that perhaps can only be made in combat.

Among the grandest Civil War memorials at Mount Auburn is the *Colossal Sphinx*. Carved in the 1870s, by Irish born sculptor, Martin Milmore, it commemorates the ending of the Civil War and of African-American slavery. The inscription on the monument reads:

American Union Preserved
African Slavery Destroyed
By the Uprising of a Great People
By the Blood of Fallen Heroes

This sculpture has a massive and timeless quality to it. An original purpose of Mount Auburn and strongly promoted by Jacob Bigelow, one of the founders, was that it should also be a repository of works of art. Bigelow, always actively involved with Mount Auburn, commissioned the *Colossal Sphinx* to integrate "the strength of the lion with the beauty and benignity of woman." An American eagle is on the sphinx's forehead and an American water lily at the base. There are other sculptures by Milmore at Mount Auburn: the *Wingate Dog*, the *Copenhagen Monument* and the *Reverend Thomas Whittemore*.

It was a unique collaboration between a member of an old New England family and an Irish immigrant. In those days, there wasn't much interaction between Irish Catholics and Yankee Protestants. Milmore was four years old when his family came to the United States and he died at the age of thirty-eight. The cause of his death is not clear. It has been suggested that he died of liver disease or tuberculosis. However, there seems to be a history of early death in the family. His father and brothers also died very young. The funeral services were held at Saint Patrick's, a Catholic Church in Roxbury (Boston), Massachusetts, on July 21, 1883. Milmore's death inspired one of Daniel Chester French's most impressive works, the Milmore Memorial, *Death Staying the Hand of the Sculptor*. French is probably best known for the *Lincoln Memorial* in Washington, D. C. The Milmore family memorial is located at Forest Hills Cemetery in Boston. It evokes the *Colossal Sphinx* by showing a young artist actually carving a sphinx, but stopped by death in mid-work.

In my life, I have had a number of casual conversations that have led me to all sorts of interests that have become very personally significant. In fact, on more than one occasion, I have wondered what would have happened if those particular conversations had never taken place. The Mount Auburn/Nathan Appleton conversation occurred in the early 1990s. This is just when I had become interested in the Civil War. Mount Auburn became more than just a place I stopped by one day to get some information about a Civil War soldier's grave. The special quality of Mount Auburn comes back in all sorts of ways, but there are some memorable moments that come to me as I write.

I am often struck by the tranquility of Mount Auburn. Just go in fifty feet from the main entrance and something special seems to descend. On one of the horticultural tours, we went into a little gully and an almost mystical feeling surrounded us. It was as though the air was holding its breath. On a perfect summer's evening walking tour, I turned away from the talk and I could have been there all by myself. There was just the slightest summer breeze and that wonderful feeling of tranquility. Yet, I was only a few feet away from a group of people. Add to that the almost miraculous ability the cemetery has to look beautiful at almost every angle. Photo opportunities abound. There always seems to be a beautiful view. How was this achieved? How can they make the whole place seem so planned and perfect, on both a horticultural and aesthetic level?

One early summer day in 2011, I was walking in Mount Auburn near the reflecting pond. I sat on a bench and directly across the water was the Mary Baker Eddy monument. I glanced to the left and up at the trees and saw the most amazing rippling light and shadows on the leaves above. It reminded me of lamps from the 1950s that somehow made an effect of movement in waterfalls, or smoke coming from old-style train engines. As a child, these lamps fascinated me, but these shadows were made by nature. The light and shadows rippled and reflected across the leaves, sent by the gently rippling water. Was that a one-time effect I happened to see? Were the conditions just right only that one time? Could it ever be reproduced? I stayed there and watched it until I had to leave.

I have participated in many of the horticultural walks and I particularly like the 7:00 A.M. walks held in the spring.

On a fall day, many years ago, I sat on a bench overlooking Consecration Dell. The weather was perfect. It was a comfortable temperature; there was wind, but just the right amount. The wind made a sound, a wonderful swishing and lively sound. I kept looking up at the trees and watched them sway. I stayed there for some time. I was writing – which I don't usually do at Mount Auburn. It evoked what it might have been like that fall day in 1831, when the cemetery was consecrated.

The history-focused talks have opened up all sorts of information about the people that now rest there.

I have grown to love this place so well that I have bought a columbarium niche in Story Chapel. Partly it was to make it easier for my family at the event of my death. However, the main reason was that I want to spend eternity in a place which is beautiful, but also where people are coming and having a good time. It is a cemetery that has serenity and joy as well as its somber duty as a burial ground.

Special thanks to Anthony Sammarco, Edward Burdekin, John Canesi, Michael Chesson, Edward Gordon, John Humphrey, and Ernest Rohdenburg III.

Colossal Sphinx, Martin Milmore. Photo by John Harrison.

Bigelow Chapel from Washington Tower. Photo by John Harrison.

Connie Biewald

Life at Mount Auburn

I have tried. I am trying. Most days I like knowing that living won't last forever. Spring, summer, winter, fall, morning, afternoon, evening, night: they begin and end, blend into each other, and I am glad that I am old enough now to know. Trust the certainty of cycles.

I have no favorite season, but I do have favorite trees. The witch hazel, for blooming when no other tree dares. The yellow blossoms command my attention against the monochrome landscape of slushy late winter. At another time of year I might overlook their slight presence, but in the muddy days when temperatures still fall below freezing, a flowering bush, fringed and delicate, presents as the wonder it is. I remember the blooms from last year when I knew they couldn't be forsythia – too early and too pale a yellow – so I slopped through the melting snow to read the tag on the trunk. A full year has passed since that day – spring, summer, fall and winter of births and deaths and narrow escapes, school lunches, ripped jeans, and bedtime stories.

I wear the black winter coat I've worn for years. Same season, same woman, same tree. I stroke the gray bark of the witch hazel and finger the damp yellow petals. My body fills with a moment of understanding, complete and satisfying, the secular faith I've been longing for. Rhythms. Patterns. Cycles. In the year since I last saw these blooms, warblers migrated north and south, frogs hibernated and emerged, corpses in their graves decomposed while my dead inhabit my dreams and memories. On the planet for fifty years, walking at Mount Auburn Cemetery regularly, I only now realize what this place offers me.

The spring thaw releases a fresh dampness from the soggy earth, different from autumn's rich leaf mold, a thin clean smell of melting and the tentative stretching of roots and stems into spongy dirt. Broken ice, at the edges of the pond, tinkles and sloshes; the ends of branches drip. Snowdrops appear on the hillside near the tower, not long after the witch hazel blooms. First one, then a few, then the hill is covered.

The next weeks bring crocuses, daffodils, and the flowering trees: magnolias with the thick waxy petals I want to bite, the pink and white clouds of ornamental fruit trees and the regal red and yellow cones of horse chestnut blossoms and the four-petaled dogwood flowers, pleasing in their simplicity. Every day more birds arrive to add their distinctive voices to the chorus of noisy arguments.

The oriole pair settles into the same willow tree they've inhabited for years, and I recognize their song. In fifth grade, we studied birds and our teacher played the calls over and over on a record player, but I never could distinguish their disembodied chirps and squawks. I need birds now, with their bright feathers and determined nest-building. I believe in them and their migration.

From a bench near the orioles' tree, on the north side of Willow Pond, I can watch the late spring breeze brush through the trees across the way, and its glittering progress along the surface of the water. A Great Blue Heron fishes in the reeds. Huge bullfrog tadpoles forage near the shore. They look as though they'd be easy to grab, but slide away before even the tips of my fingers get wet.

When the bluets emerge, vivid among the grass and ground cover, summer is not far off. I stare at a patch that surrounds the elephantine foot of the beech tree near the cemetery entrance. I can't find words to describe their deep purple-blue color and wish I painted or took photographs instead of having to resort to the inadequacy of black markings on a white page.

Summer transforms the weeping beech trees into lush hiding places, their low branches, crooked and thick, perfect for contemplation. An occasional bird trills, the briefest lilting melody over the steady thrum and buzz of insects. Ducks float on the surface of the pond. The air hangs heavy. Turtles on logs, bake in the sun. Who knew so many shades of green existed? Dragonflies hover. Bright, sleek frogs with gold eyes that peer above the water line, leap as I come close, bodies landing with a plop in deeper spots. The bullfrogs croak in deep musical conversation I think I understand. Red-tailed Hawks circle high above. The kingfisher swoops from one favorite tree to another with a rattly cry.

In the fall, the sourwood turns a stunning combination of red and yellow, and the split-leaf Japanese maple burns bright. On the path, overlooking Consecration Dell, I spot a streak of rusty orange amidst the ferns. When it emerges from the green, a red fox stands on the path three yards away and looks at me – stretches, stares, stretches again and trots off.

After rain, mushrooms and toadstools pop up in surprising places. Seeds and seedpods crunch under foot – the only ones I recognize are acorns and the long beanlike pods of the locust tree. The gingko drops its smelly yellow fruit and fanlike leaves. The little girl in me imagines acorn cap plates, leafy placemats and pine needle brooms in the kitchens of moss-carpeted fairy houses. The goldening leaves of the weeping beech cling to the drooping, twisted branches, long after other trees are bare. The frogs blanket themselves in mud, heartbeats slowing. They will spend the cold months, half frozen, breathing through their skin.

In the still of winter, sun low in the sky, even at noon, the ice-encrusted branches of the oak trees glitter. Later, naked and dark, they scratch the blue of the sky. I love the stillness, the restful grays and browns and muted greens. Only the skittering of squirrels on tree bark breaks the silence. In the late afternoon, the sky is silver. Nothing moves near the iced-over ponds.

I have seen these changes again and again, collected crimson leaves with my children, ducked under the diminutive orange maple, foliage drenched in the glow of the late afternoon sun, admired the crescent moon caught in the black and bony fingers of a winter treetop, breathed in the heavy scent of lilacs, kissed my husband in the green space beneath the weeping beech. I have seen a coyote sitting on its haunches up high on a ridge and held my breath waiting for it to yelp or howl, but it stood and slipped away between the gravestones.

Gravestones. It's a cemetery full of them. I love the angels in winter with snow on their heads and wings. I read the names out loud. I make up stories about them. They make me wonder. How many of the folks now underground walked these very paths holding hands or peering through binoculars? And the dates. I do the subtraction. Compare their time on the surface with my own. I wonder how many more times I will watch the heron spear a fish or pinch a baby turtle in its beak.

I find the grave of a man born the same year I was, who died when he was thirty. If I'd died at thirty, I would have missed the best years of my life. Will I climb the tower with grandchildren, the way I did with my sons when they were small? How many of the children buried here once raced up and down the stairs pretending to be knights or dragons? How many rose up from behind gravestones, arms stuck out straight, knees locked, pretending to be zombies? In the days when so many died young, children were better behaved than that, so perhaps not many, maybe none. Today, though living parents attempt to shush their kids' exuberant shouts, I enjoy their unrestrained appreciation of this place.

Famous folks are buried here, but I prefer the graves of those I don't know. Once, right in front of a stone marked "Savage," I stood still for more than an hour, watching a hawk eviscerate a squirrel. A husband's granite column reads, "Best Beloved." Beside it stands the wife's, my favorite. "She tried."

Savor the moments. Trust the cycles. Trying is the best we can do.

It's enough.

Photo by John Harrison.

Sandy Selesky

Scarlet Tanager

Song Sparrow

Brown Creeper

Cedar Waxwing　　　　　*House Wren*

Cape May Warbler

Magnolia Warbler

Black-throated Green Warbler

Black-and-white Warbler

Green Heron with frog

Wood Thrush

Baltimore Oriole

Hooded Mergansers

Red-tailed Hawk on Mary Baker Eddy Memorial

Yellow-rumped Warbler

Linda Darman

Walk with Me

Enter through iron gates.

VISITORS ARE
WELCOME
America's First
Landscaped Cemetery
Consecrated in 1831
A National Historic Landmark

It's a cloudy day but the heat has broken and the Japanese clethra are in bloom. Walk with me. Down Fountain Avenue to Halcyon Path and Halcyon Lake, surrounded by weeping willows.

Mary Baker Eddy
Discoverer and Founder of Christian Science
Author of Science and Health with Key to the Scriptures

The architecture of her monument echoes that of the Mother Church on Boston's Massachusetts Avenue. Stately columns and a domed roof. One July night, after a performance at Symphony Hall, we strolled over to the Christian Science Center, then sat in the fragrant humid air by the I. M. Pei reflecting pool, talking for hours.

Walk with me. Through tiny, sloped Lilac Path.

GARDNER

Her mausoleum is as stark as the Venetian villa of the Isabella Stewart Gardner Museum is ornate. On an unseasonably hot day last April we walked to the museum and rested in the cool courtyard, awed by the annual hanging of nasturtiums. Magnificent ribbons of orange and yellow reaching two stories to the ground. Nasturtiums were my grandmother's favorite flower.

Central Avenue. Fannie Farmer, America's first celebrity chef, lies next to William Fredrick Harnden, "Founder of the Express Business in America." This he accomplished in a short lifetime. "He died 14 Jan 1845. 31 years." Presumably, it is his trusty dog, rendered in stone, that protects his gravesite. But here is the grave we have come to see.

–MERRITT–
FARMER–PERKINS

My copy of *The Fannie Farmer Cookbook*, Eleventh Edition, is in tatters. Mother gave it to me when I moved out on my own. Our hometown food authority following me from Boston to my New York apartment, encouraging me to "develop good cooking habits" and "maintain a pleasing balance between contrasting textures, colors, and tastes."

Across Central Avenue are five tiny stones set in a perfect row perpendicular to the road and to the rows of other gravestones. "Father," "Lydia," and "Emily," and two others, the names erased by years of exposure to the elements. Presumably Mother and another child. Another girl? Did they all tread as lightly on this earth as the modesty of their graves implies?

Here is the Dell. You took me here when the baby owls were born. It was the first time the owls had successfully bred in the cemetery and the fact that the nest was so visible was an extremely rare occurrence in and of itself. The excitement among the birders that day was something to behold. You stood behind me holding binoculars to my eyes until I was able to spot the two small furry mounds sticking up from the nest. One night many years earlier, the kids' pre-school arranged an outing into the Northern Massachusetts woods to see the owls. Tiptoeing, shushing the children, stifling laughter, until we came to the clearing. Standing in silence, we followed the direction of the teacher's outstretched arm as he pointed toward the clump of trees where we could expect to see that mysterious bird. And then, after more than an hour with no sighting, the children exhausted and cranky, we all trudged back to our cars, the disappointment evident in our step.

Walk with me onto Walnut Avenue. Here lie Samuel C. Bishop and his wife Sarah. Samuel died on Independence Day in 1872. An imposing stone sheaf of wheat covers the top of the long white monument. And at the bottom these words: "The harvest is ripe; its fruits are gathered." That says it all.

Along Bellwort Path, past the mountain laurel. Past the astute Fuller family, with its notable representatives, a clan so large that their plot reaches from Bellwort to Pyrola. And then to the monument topped by a large elaborate urn.

Sacred to the Memory of
CHARLES BULFINCH
Born in Boston
AD 1763
Graduated Harvard College
AD 1781
Chairman of the Selectmen of Boston

from 1799–1817
Architect of the State House of Massachusetts
from 1795–1798
And of the Capitol of the United States
from 1815–1830
He died April 15, 1844

In the 1960s Mother spent a summer in the iconic 1823 Bulfinch Building of Massachusetts General Hospital, the nine small rooms on the lower level having been dedicated to unusual cases. Her floor-mates included a giant and one of the rare cases of Gillian Barre syndrome. We visited every evening, sitting on wrought iron furniture on the sloping lawn in front of the building. That lawn is still there, a small patch of green surrounded by the towering glass and steel hospital buildings erected all around it in the years since. Mother's illness was studied and researched and then her case was presented in the old Bulfinch surgical amphitheater known as the Ether Dome, doctors peppering her with questions from the rows of straight-backed nineteenth-century bleacher-style seats.

Walk with me along winding Mound Avenue, past the young couple planning their life together – the names of future children and even the dog. Talk of lives that have not yet begun, here among those that ended long ago.

Then to Meadow Road. Beyond the wall. Just before Flicker Path. An open lawn with rows of small stones lying flat on the ground.

MINOR WHITE
All the way to Heaven
is heaven, for he said
I am the way
1908–1976

You keep your pajamas in Minor's old wooden trunk. Our friends Wayne and David were both professional photographers and students of Minor White, the noted photographer and educator and one of the founders of *Aperture* magazine. He was their spiritual teacher as well as photography mentor. David inherited Minor's antique trunk, and when he moved to Hawaii he gave it to us.

PARSONS
Emily E.
Mar. 8, 1824
May 19, 1880

One name in a long list of Parsons engraved on the worn obelisk. Emily was the founder of Mount Auburn Hospital in Cambridge. In the early 1980s the midwives at the hospital turned one room of the maternity ward into one of the first so-called "birthing rooms." Yellow walls, floral print curtains, and a sofa next to the hospital bed. Autumn came overnight that Labor Day weekend, the heat giving way to cool temperatures by morning. A single patch of bright orange could be seen in the tree outside the birthing room window. A baby boy was born.

It's getting late. The participants in tonight's Twilight Art Stroll are gathering in front of Story Chapel. Horticulturalists, birders, historians, biographers, hikers all flock to the oldest landscaped cemetery in the country…to pursue their interests…to commune with nature or with the spirits…or just for the memories. A cemetery is, after all, in the business of memories.

Dan Shaughnessy

Hi, Neighbor. Have a 'Gansett.

Curt Gowdy grew up in Wyoming and entitled his biography *Cowboy at the Mike*. He was the first sportscaster to win a Peabody Award; was a member of twenty halls of fame; and broadcast sixteen World Series, nine Super Bowls, eight Olympics, twelve Rose Bowls and twenty-four NCAA Final Fours. He broadcast baseball's national *Game of the Week* for its first ten years and hosted *The American Sportsman* on ABC for two decades.

When major league baseball and professional football proliferated on television in the 1960s and 1970s, Gowdy was the network voice of sports. He was the most famous sports broadcaster in the land. He belonged to all of America.

But we know better. Curt Gowdy belongs to New England. He belongs to the Red Sox. He's the man who made "Hi, Neighbor, Have a 'Gansett!" part of our local language, no less than "The Midnight Ride of Paul Revere." And that's why it's fitting that Gowdy is buried in Mount Auburn Cemetery with so many other gods of regional folklore.

Gowdy was the voice of the Red Sox from 1951 through 1965. He spread the gospel of Ted Williams and introduced fans to a young Carl Yastrzemski. He promoted the "Jimmy Fund," and urged our dads to grab a cold can of Narragansett beer after they came in from mowing the lawn.

The Red Sox of the Gowdy years were nothing like the Sox of today. There was no string of sellouts, no "Sweet Caroline" after the top half of the eighth, no three World Championships and no Monster Seats atop the left field wall. The Sox played bad baseball in front of small crowds, sometimes less than one thousand fans. They had Don Buddin making errors at shortstop and Gene Conley abandoning the team in mid-road trip and buying a plane ticket to Jerusalem. They were a country club, a clown show, and – disgracefully – the last major league to promote an African-American player to the big leagues (Pumpsie Green, 1959). The Sox lost one hundred games in 1965, Gowdy's final year as club broadcaster.

Baby Boomer fans remember little success or dignity from this era. But we knew we had the best baseball broadcaster. Curt Gowdy was the real deal. His honey voice was the sound of summer, the last thing we heard at night before falling asleep in the late innings of another Red Sox loss. "Curt Gowdy was the voice under the pillow," said Dr. Charles Steinberg, club choreographer for the Red Sox in the twenty-first century.

Gowdy was born in Green River, Wyoming, in 1919, ten months after the Red Sox won the 1918 World Series. Basketball was his first love and he was good enough to start for the University of Wyoming. Like many announcers, he started out broadcasting sparsely attended high school football games. He received no professional training. He was hired by a CBS affiliate in Oklahoma City in 1946 and three years later was selected from a field of three hundred entrants as Mel Allen's partner on Yankee broadcasts. In 1951, he was hired by the Red Sox and quickly became a favorite of owner Thomas Yawkey and slugger Ted Williams.

Gowdy was at the microphone when Williams came to the plate for his final at bat in the big leagues on September 28, 1960. In his essay on that game – "Hub Fans Bid Kid Adieu" – esteemed author John Updike described Gowdy's "ever so soothing and sensible voice, with its guileless hint of Wyoming twang." Williams homered and Gowdy made the call.

"It was one of the big thrills of my life," Gowdy said later. "He hit that ball and I saw it start to soar and get some distance. I got all excited and I said, 'It's going, going, gone!' and then I stopped and said, 'Ted Williams has hit a home run in his last time at bat in the major leagues."

Williams and Gowdy became close friends in their golden years. It was not unusual to see them talking fishing or appearing jointly to promote the Jimmy Fund. Gowdy enjoyed bragging that his friend Teddy Ballgame was "the best hitter, the best pilot, and the best fisherman that ever lived."

Just as Curt Gowdy was the best broadcaster who ever lived.

Our Curt Gowdy.

Hi, Neighbor. Have a 'Gansett.

Yellow Warbler. Photo by John Harrison.

Peter Filichia

A Day with the Dean

John Harrison, the co-editor of this book, has been my oldest and dearest friend since our grammar school days during the Eisenhower Administration. Once he became a Mount Auburn devotee, he soon mentioned that "Elliot Norton is buried here."

And sure enough, on one of our spins around Mount Auburn while John was on the lookout for birds, I spotted the modest stone rectangle at the bottom of a totem pole's worth of other stone rectangles.

"NORTON W. Elliot May 17, 1903 – July 20, 2003"

Norton was often called the "Dean of American Drama Critics," for many a new play or musical made a point of coming to Boston before braving Broadway simply to get his opinion in the *Record-American*. He also had a weekly TV show on WGBH – *Eliot Norton Reviews* – on which he interviewed those who'd worked on the production he'd seen the previous night. As Neil Simon recalled in his 1996 memoir *Rewrites,* when he appeared on the program after the opening of his new play, *The Odd Couple*, Norton gave him a suggestion on how to improve his third act. Simon immediately knew that Norton was right and took his advice. Ever since then, Simon has always insisted that Norton's idea made the difference between a modest success and a smash hit. In other words, without Norton's wise words, "He's a Felix and I'm an Oscar" might not have become an oft-heard expression that respectively contrasts cleanliness with slovenliness.

Many of us like to say to our friends "May you live to be a hundred!" Those who said it to Norton had their wish come true. As William Goldman wrote in *The Season,* his 1969 landmark book about Broadway, "Drama critics live a long time."

I hope he's right. I'm a drama critic, too.

I started in 1968 for my college newspaper and the following year was recruited to write for *Boston after Dark,* a weekly paper that was the forerunner of what is now the *Boston Phoenix.* During the last weekend of August 1969, my editor called me in to give me an atypical assignment.

"That new play *Hello and Goodbye* that's coming to Theatre Company of Boston next Monday for a week?" he asked without waiting for me to answer. "Well, with Labor Day, we have to go to press earlier than our Tuesday deadline. There's only one way we can get in a review for Wednesday's paper, and that's to send you to Paramus, New Jersey, where the show is playing *this* week. They do a Thursday matinee, so go up, see it, come back and file your review as soon as you can. How old are you now?"

That last line might seem to be a non-sequitur, but I knew what he meant. At that time Eastern Airlines had a "Youth Fare" which allowed those twenty-two and younger to fly at half-price.

"Twenty-three," I had to admit, which got a scowl in return. That meant that my round-trip fare would cost the company $32 and not $16. But my editor wanted the review, so off to Logan Airport I went that balmy Thursday morning. And who was at the airport gate but Eliot Norton?

Did I dare approach the great man? Sure! We were undoubtedly on the same mission, so he'd probably be amenable to discussing it. And indeed, when I introduced myself as the *Boston after Dark* critic who would be reviewing *Hello and Goodbye,* he gave me a big smile, waved a welcoming hand to the empty seat next to him, and we were off and talking. Although his newspaper was a daily, he'd intended to take a long Labor Day weekend, so he was going to New Jersey in order to write his review in advance and enjoy his holiday.

Given that I'd been going to the theater for all of eight years – and Norton had been a critic for a solid thirty-five – I had plenty to ask him before, during and after the flight. "Tell me about the opening night of *Harvey,* when it had its world premiere in Boston," I implored. "When theatergoers saw Elwood motioning that Harvey should precede him into a room, they must have assumed it was a person to whom he was speaking. When his sister later told a doctor 'He's a rabbit,' the audience had to explode with laughter – for they never would have assumed that." Norton's smile alone let me see that the reaction was as titanic as I'd surmised. He then went on to tell me what I didn't know: when the play opened at the now-defunct Copley Theatre, it was called *The Pooka;* it wasn't renamed *Harvey* until halfway through the Boston run.

Then I asked, "When *South Pacific* tried out at the Shubert, what was the Boston Brahmin audience's reaction when they heard 'You've got to be carefully taught' – a plea for racial tolerance?" Norton's eyes widened and he took me through the silence that the first-nighters gave the song. They certainly didn't agree that that nice young man from Main Line Philadelphia should take up with a Polynesian girl. However, he said, their refusal to applaud the song didn't sway Rodgers and Hammerstein in the least; they never considered dropping the controversial song, for it conveyed the point they most wanted to make. "And if the show didn't succeed because of it," Norton said, "they still would have been proud for having tried to open prejudiced minds."

Norton clearly enjoyed that I, forty-three years younger, wanted to know about the theatrical past and wasn't just interested in what was happening here and now. Perhaps my thirst to hear every theatrical story reminded him of himself way back when. That could explain his inviting me to join him for the lunch he'd arranged in advance with *Hello and Goodbye*'s producer, Kermit Bloomgarden.

Wow! Bloomgarden was the original producer of *Death of a Salesman, The Diary of Anne Frank* and *The Crucible* – not to mention *The Music Man.* Legend had it that on opening night of that last-named hit, first-nighters were so enraptured by "Seventy-Six Trombones" that they'd started clapping in rhythm in the middle of the number. Was this true, I asked both men over my veal piccata, or just a press agent's white lie to drum up business? From the way that both Bloomgarden and Norton gave a single simultaneous vigorous and definitive head nod, I now knew for sure that it was true.

Another thrill awaited me when Norton arranged for my seat to be changed so that I could sit next to him at the theater. Before the lights went down, he asked me what some of my favorite theatrical experiences were. My mention of Zoe Caldwell in *The Prime of Miss Jean Brodie,* Tammy Grimes in *The Unsinkable Molly Brown,* Alan Arkin in *Luv* and Barbara Harris in *On a Clear Day You Can See Forever* all got nods of approval.

I knew I couldn't go wrong in mentioning *I Never Sang for My Father,* for I'd remembered his reaction from the tryout at the Colonial: "At last, after months of waiting, the American theater has a drama of real distinction." I hadn't memorized all of his reviews, but this one I knew, because I had managed to invest in the Broadway production. (Would that the New York critics could have agreed with him! I lost every penny.)

And then the curtain opened on *Hello and Goodbye* by up-and-coming South African playwright Athol Fugard. It told of Johnny and Hester, a brother and sister who hadn't seen each other in years; now they were going through their deceased father's belongings.

Even the great Colleen Dewhurst couldn't make it interesting, although her playing against a dull actor certainly didn't help. But in the end, nothing much happened. Hester left empty-handed and so, I thought, did the audience.

Of course during intermission and on our way to the airport, Norton and I didn't discuss the show. He spent much of the time telling me about his battles with Lee and J.J. Shubert, erstwhile producers and theater owners who once had a stranglehold on Broadway – and drove him crazy by second-guessing and criticizing his reviews for many years.

We arrived at Logan and said a fond goodbye. I went to the men's room, and while there, thought of another brilliant performance I should have mentioned: Betty Field, who'd played the hapless Amanda Wingfield in a 1964 production of *The Glass Menagerie* at the Charles Playhouse. Now, more than five years later, I could still see her trying to make the best of a bad situation in her job as what we now call a telemarketer, desperately trying to sell magazine subscriptions and expressing her complete joy and gratitude when she finally made a sale. I vividly recall her always maintaining her optimism while firmly rebutting her daughter Laura when the lass described herself as "a cripple" – until the play's penultimate scene, when Amanda herself in frustration spit out the word "cripple" right in front of the girl. I could still hear the gasp I emitted.

In fact, even now, I still can. Moreover, if you and I went into the Charles Playhouse right now, I could take you to the row and seat that I occupied that April night more than a half-century ago – not because I actually know the row's letter or seat number, but because Fields and *The Glass Menagerie* made such a devastating impression on me I know where I was sitting. Too bad I'd forgotten to mention this unforgettable performance to Norton, whose review of it I'd missed.

But lo and behold, when I came out and walked out of the airport, there he was at curbside waiting for a cab. Wonderful! I had my second chance!

He spied me and smiled, which was enough to make me go up to him and say, "Oh, there's one other performance I'll never forget." He smiled in anticipation until I said "Betty Field in *The Glass Menagerie.*"

The smile immediately disappeared and was replaced by a furious scowl. "Oh, Betty Field was utterly ridiculous in that! Ridiculous!" he erupted, full not only of criticism but also genuine anger. "She was a caricature of Amanda! A cartoon! An abomination!"

A cab came, and Norton got in without offering me a ride. I hadn't yet heard the theatrical dictum "Always leave 'em wanting more," but I learned a variation on the theme that day. If I'd only quit while I'd been ahead! All my efforts to impress the "Dean" had now all gone for naught.

What I hadn't yet learned was that the original Broadway production in 1945 contained what is still perceived to be one of the greatest performances in Broadway history: Laurette Taylor's Amanda. Perhaps one reason Norton felt Field could do no right was that he'd seen Taylor do no wrong.

I went home and wrote my review and in those ancient days before e-mail, drove it to the office. It was then typeset and was published on Wednesday.

Only one problem: during the Paramus run, Bloomgarden hadn't been any more pleased with the actor playing opposite Dewhurst than I was. Even as we were having lunch, he and director Barney Simon must have been negotiating with up-and-coming actor Martin Sheen to replace the performer. Now that Sheen had agreed, the play would need additional rehearsals. So instead of coming to Boston, it would head to New York and rehearse right up until previews on September 11 and its opening on September 18.

My published review was a lame duck. If Norton ever wrote a review, his daily paper with a less stringent deadline was able to kill it before it ran.

Precisely a week later, I attended the opening of *The Iceman Cometh* at that same Charles Playhouse where Field had enthralled me. The theater had been reconfigured to a thrust stage; I was in the second row on the right hand side when I saw Elliot Norton enter and take his seat in the center section.

Given my less-than-Field-day experience, I didn't know whether to look at him and smile or just thrust my head into my program. I was relieved when the lights went down, and when they came up for the first intermission, I quickly got up and headed to the men's room so that he wouldn't see me.

But eventually I had to return to my seat, and when I did, I found Elliot Norton waiting for me there. "I read your review," he said. "And you know, I felt very much the way that you did. Well done!"

Such a man deserves to live to be a hundred.

Photo by John Harrison.

Eric Smith

American Redstart

Red Fox

Red Fox

Red Fox

Merlin

Eastern Towhee

Gary Goshgarian

Recollections Among the Dead

There are places in the world that offer a sumptuous appeal to the eyes, whose landscapes imbue memories of ponds, wooded lanes, the roll of the grassy slopes, the bursts of color, the flash of birds and fauna. A place to which our daydreams return in distant and harsher times, warming our hearts, filling us with yearnings and fleeting joy. Mount Auburn Cemetery is such a special place for me. It's where I courted Kathleen who would later become my wife of more than thirty years. It's a green world where we later brought our two sons to glimpse some glories of nature.

Yes, a cemetery is an odd venue for romance to bud. But "Sweet Auburn," as it is affectionately known, is not your everyday burying ground. It's a park, a patch of wilderness in the city, an extensive arboretum, the resting place of august New England personages, and a glorious garden where one can sleep out eternity.

It's also where my love life began – and so many stirring memories.

Back then, Kathy lived in a nearby apartment block on Mount Auburn Street, a wide and busy artery for cars, trucks and buses, where the din was constant, and the air was laced with exhaust fumes. (Still is.) But it was no more than a ten minute walk to

"Sweet Auburn," which was "wilderness *enau*" for young lovers – and old lovers still.

Back then we had a few favorite benches to take in the pleasures of the place. One was by the somber gravestone block of Henry Wadsworth Longfellow, one of America's favorite nineteenth-century poets. As young – some would say "hokey" – English teachers, we'd read passages from his poems, *Evangeline*, *The Song of Hiawatha*, and a favorite, "It's Not Always May" which ends with the reminder that, in those salad days of ours, seemed to address other people.

> Maiden, that read'st this simple rhyme,
> Enjoy thy youth, it will not stay;
> Enjoy the fragrance of thy prime,
> For oh, it is not always May!

> Enjoy the Spring of Love and Youth,
> To some good angel leave the rest;
> For Time will teach thee soon the truth,
> There are no birds in last year's nest!

Or we'd hang out at the burial spot of "that magnificent Yankee," Oliver Wendell Holmes, Jr. Befitting a Supreme Court Justice, his is a solid and austere headstone that sits on a tree-covered slope across from a wide rolling green field that hinted at eternity. In springtime, flowering dogwoods would hang over the site like a canopy of a million butterflies.

Although some five thousand trees and seven hundred different species occupy the acreage of "Sweet Auburn," our favorite place to idle was under the canopy of a towering redwood rising a few yards from the incredible monument of Mary Baker Eddy, founder of the Church of Christ, Scientist. Built beside lovely tree-lined Halcyon Lake, that splendid white-stoned neoclassical temple is a pillared rotunda, resembling that of the fourth century BCE Sanctuary of Athena at Delphi. Or perhaps some other whited memorial as in "Tempe or the dales of Arcady?" where like the Grecian urn in John Keats' ode the "silent form dost tease us out of thought / As doth eternity." But we didn't have eternity, and before the trees went bare, this bold lover kissed his maiden fair many a times in the shadows of that structure.

But another and far more banal attraction found us returning to that monument. It had been rumored that Ms. Eddy had been buried with a telephone in her tomb. So we'd sit on a bench and soak in the beauty while half-waiting for a dial tone to fill the air. In spite of the fact that the story was something of an urban – or graveyard – legend, we amused ourselves speculating why she had done that. Did she distrust her undertaker, fearing premature burial? Or was she certain that she'd be resurrected and call friends from the other side? If so, was her spirit capable of dialing a pre-push-button phone? Or did this grand proponent of spiritual self-healing manage to defy the conquering worm and come back some Lady Lazarus? Or a pious zombie? We had fun imagining the phone ringing and a tiny female voice rising from under the marble, "Sorry, wrong number."

In all truth, Ms. Eddy had not really been buried with a telephone. During the construction of her monument, one had been installed for security guards at the site. And from that, rumors flew. None of them true, but we had our time with them.

Over the years Kathy and I still went back to commune with the spectacular sylvan lushness of the place. Then as time passed, with a stroller. It was in the shadows of that sylvan temple where our sons practiced walking – more like duck-waddling – across the grass. Then, as the years progressed, they chased after Canada geese and went mucking at the water's edge for frogs and salamanders. Later still we explored the grottos and fields in hopes of glimpsing raccoons, groundhogs and foxes. And we did, as well as the now-ubiquitous Red-tailed Hawks and, on two occasions, a Great Horned Owl. Later still we jogged through the lanes with our boys, who first pumped their little legs to keep up with us, then, all too soon, burning us in long-legged sprints.

And we watched the grand variety of birds, not sure if that was a Baltimore Oriole or a Scarlet Tanager. And we watched the clutches of dedicated birders with their industrial-strength tripods and no-nonsense scopes and Roger Tory Peterson field guides in their back pockets. And we listened as the air filled with cicada clicks of camera shutters behind lenses the size of baseball bats.

Now one of my sons goes there with tripods and lenses of his own to shoot birds and celebrity coyotes with names like Big Caesar, patriarch of the clan, and his mate Czarina, bestowed upon them by devoted fan and photographer John Harrison and Camilla Fox, founder of Project Coyote.

Like thousands of others who have "Sweet Auburn" in their hearts, Kathy and I still go there on occasion – for a momentary reprieve from the concrete-poured world and swirl of steel; to take in the splendid flora and fauna; to snap off a few photos; to admire the sculptured resting places of New England notables. And, of course, to recapture sweet memories of our fragrant primes.

Sweet Auburn, you give death a good name.

Nathan Goshgarian

Wild Turkey

Red-tailed Hawk

Red-tailed Hawk

Red-tailed Hawk

Pierce Butler

The Reality of Birds

I had my first encounter with a Worm-eating Warbler just below the tower where Rose and Violet Paths come together at one of the entrances to the Dell. Or rather I heard its reedy rattle with the appropriate combination of awe and amazement. Could it be? I wondered. Or am I getting it mixed up with a Chipping Sparrow? Bird calls have never been my strength. I have to relearn those of the warblers I'm most likely to encounter at Mount Auburn each year, and the Worm-eating is listed as 'uncommon.' I looked around for some more experienced birder to corroborate my guess, but there was no one. I was alone – with no more than a suspicion of the bird's presence.

But when I turned on to Amaranth Path and ascended the little mound of the Harvard Corporation Lot, there was the bird, working the low branches of an oak, shockingly close, all its markings visible to the naked eye. After I had confirmed the sighting with a hasty glance at my Petersen, I backed away from the bird, partly in order to train my binoculars on it with ease, but mostly because I felt that I was too close. You'll surely spook it, I said to myself. I retreated until I came up against the Harvard monument (upon which I had often rested arms tired from watching warblers flitting about the high branches of the trees surrounding the Dell). There I took my stand and observed the bird at my leisure.

I watched it for a good twenty minutes without interruption, which seemed to me an inordinately long time to have such a bird at my disposal. As I watched it, I became aware of the bird in a way that was different from my hurried apprehension of the scores of warblers that flit through my binocular view during spring migration. This was a respite from the eager grasping at outline and color, the shuffling of names and behaviors, the impatience to arrive at an identification – in order to rush on to the next. There was only one bird, one moment, or rather a succession of moments containing the bird, each sufficient and complete in itself.

I'd always considered the Worm-eating an unlovely warbler, remarkable perhaps for its odd call and its relative scarcity, but certainly not on a par with such stars of the air as the Blackburnian, the Prothonotary, and the Cerulean, whose very names evoked their brilliant and usually fleeting presence. But I began to see – as the moments passed and the bird with the undignified name continued to oblige – that the Worm-eating had its own claim to my attention. The plumage has been described as drab (with the exception of the yellow throat and head that were not particularly striking in this member of the species), but I was discovering many subtle shades of color in the wings and back. The head was elegantly striped and produced a curious effect when seen from in front and slightly above, as though the bird were wearing a kind of helmet. And there was its indescribable and unique manner, which no doubt contributes to the first impression, but becomes more apparent when you have the opportunity to 'hang out' with the bird: the trembling of the tail while making the call, the wide straining beak like a chick eager to be fed, the deft foraging of leaves and spearing of grubs in the bark.

I also became aware of certain changes in myself, the observer, as we continued to 'hang out' together, the bird and I. In the field, I'm as competitive as the next birder. I want to see every warbler that's out there during the brief weeks of migration, and I want to add to my life list, if at all possible. I'd already added the Worm-eating, but I noticed that I was not hurrying off to try for the Tennessee that had been listed on the bulletin board at the Mount Auburn Street gate. Instead I was beginning to realize, not without a feeling of discomfort, that the state in which I normally engage in bird-watching is a harried, impatient, and amazingly enough, inattentive state. I come to Mount Auburn to watch birds, and I look forward to the spring migration as a marker of the end of the academic year and the gateway to the more leisurely summer activities of research, reading for pleasure, and writing. But while I'm in the cemetery, I'm so preoccupied with getting "good looks" at what is there that I'm hardly aware of my surroundings. And once I get a good look, I file it away for future reference, a checkmark on a list, a number and name opposite a date, and I'm off in search of the next good look. Worst of all is the sense of frustration with which I sometimes leave the cemetery, constrained by time, by fatigue, by the ten thousand errands of life, but unable to rest satisfied with what I have seen – for perhaps the simple reason that I have not really *seen* it!

Why, I might as well be shooting the birds and putting them in a bag, I said, for all the real pleasure that I get out of them! These unpleasant feelings, however, were temporarily in abeyance. I was really seeing the Worm-eating (which remarkably continued to flit about, virtually at eye-level, and in such a way that I did not have to alter my position or leave the monument against which I was leaning) and at the same time I was aware of myself and the world that I shared with the bird, of the shapes and movements of trees, of the shadowy declivity of the Dell, of the steps that led up to the stubby finger of the tower emerging above the tree tops. In the present moment, there was more than enough to occupy me, and the birds I had seen in the past or might see in the future were of no consequence.

I remember a visit I made to Mount Auburn at a time when I regarded birds as no more than a sort of pleasant amorphous background noise. I was a student, I had no career or family responsibilities to speak of, and I immediately perceived that the cemetery was, as the text accompanying the gatehouse map claims, a special place, a refuge from the hurrying world outside its gates, an environment in which one might find refreshment and renewal. Guided by the map, I discovered the tower and the Dell, Spectacle and Willow Ponds, the familiar yet unexpected names on monuments and gravestones (as diverse as the sister of Charles Stewart Parnell, Ireland's "Uncrowned King," and the brother of Lincoln's assassin), and marveled at the exotic plantings. Yet in all my peregrinations about Mount Auburn's paths and avenues, I retained the sense of its unique character – and an awareness of myself in the midst of its beauty. Why should a new interest in birding have caused this to change?

My introduction to bird-watching took place in Loxahatchee Wildlife Refuge in Florida, where my wife and I, virgin birders, saw at least two dozen birds we had never seen before in a couple of hours of walking the trails. My senses glutted with marvels, I scorned to join the birders clustered around a misplaced Kinglet – while wonders like Wood Stork and Limpkin abounded! But it wasn't long before I caught the bug that required me to list and record – and to spend hours looking for a small drab bird that had lost its way, while in a tree above my head roosted majestically the pale Florida morph of the Red-tailed Hawk.

Once in the Dell I spent some time with an elderly couple who quietly intoned a litany of the birds that were present that day – without once raising their binoculars. The binoculars were just a habit, they said; they were birding by ear. They were moving slowly, disposed to let nature come to them. They seated themselves on a coping by the water's edge, and pretty soon there was a Wilson's in a bush beside them. They were kind enough to identify some calls for me, including the mouse-like cheeping of a Blue-gray Gnatcatcher – a bird I had never seen. (Of course I saw it very shortly thereafter; it is hard not to see a bird if you know its call.) Their lesson had to do with accepting what nature offers. If the bird is not visible, can you be satisfied with the call? Not knowing what is making the call, isn't it enough to just hear it – in such a place as Mount Auburn?

I have a dear friend who will watch just about anything avian that enters his field of vision – for hours on end. It may help that he is a photographer (and a good one), but I've noticed that among the photos he sends me, sparrows are almost as well represented as warblers. And why shouldn't they be? I say. Your common house sparrow is a remarkable-looking bird – if it were not so common. But there's the rub: we are subject to the deadening influence of habit upon the senses, so that the ecstatic experience of the first encounter is not to be repeated. Or is it? I regard my friend's state almost as that of a *bodhisattva*; it is one that I can only aspire to emulate. Is my first experience of the birds of Loxahatchee beyond recall? Must my Worm-eating Warbler inevitably lose something of its aura when next I encounter it? Well, perhaps not. It may be that every day can provide the experience of "virgin birding" if the *sine qua non* is not an influx of previously unseen species, but an inner adjustment, a tuning of my senses to the reality of the birds that *are* seen.

Birds inhabit the same world as myself, but if I'm not aware of this, then birds are there only to be cataloged, collected, added to the life list. If I marvel at them, it is as aerial oddities rather than as fellow creatures with whom I share a predilection for the remarkable world that is Mount Auburn. I think of myself as somehow permanently established here; the birds are the migrants after all. But in truth this is something else that we share: I am no less a migrant, only passing through, as the changing seasons – and the monuments all around – ought to remind me. When I open myself to all that I share with birds, wonders are possible. Who if given a choice would not prefer this expanded awareness, the inclusive apperception of bird and self and world, an equanimity that savors what is unique in experience?

After the New Zealand writer Katherine Mansfield died of tuberculosis at the age of thirty-five at the Gurdjieff Institute in Fontainbleau, a young Lithuanian woman who had befriended her was walking along a passage in the old chateau when a small bird (she does not say what kind) entered at an open window, flew twice about her, and then departed. Since the tradition of her country holds that the dead revisit the living in the form of birds, she knew at once that all was well with her friend and was comforted.

In James Joyce's *Portrait of the Artist as a Young Man,* Stephen Dedalus reflects upon the portents carried by birds and remembers Swedenborg's writing "of how the creatures of the air have their knowledge and know their times and seasons because they, unlike man, are in the order of life and have not perverted that order by reason."

There are many things we might know from birds if only we would attend to them as creatures with whom we share the same world. And how could we know these things were it not for a place to which we and the birds are drawn where we can encounter them in all the immediacy of their being? Mount Auburn is such a place.

Blue-Gray Gnatcatcher. Photo by John Harrison.

Mount Auburn Rarities

By John Harrison

Northern Flicker with probable condition xanthrochromism

Northern Flicker with probable condition xanthrochromism

Fork-tailed Flycatcher (first sighting 2014)

Fork-tailed Flycatcher

Robin with condition Leucism

Robin with condition Leucism

Osprey dive at Auburn Lake

Osprey dive at Auburn Lake

Osprey dive at Auburn Lake

Northern Saw-whet Owl

White-winged Dove

Katherine Hall Page

Sweet Auburn's Shades

I love birds, but I'm not a birdwatcher. I love plants, trees and shrubs, but I'm not a horticulturalist. What brings me to Mount Auburn is the chance to visit with old friends, both those known to me only through words and those I knew face-to-face. As I wander the paths and avenues, their gravesites are mnemonics, evoking remembrances, both real and imagined.

In her wonderful guidebook, *Literary Trail of Greater Boston*, Susan Wilson's tour of Mount Auburn describes how the cemetery got its name. Harvard students, notably Emerson, used to trek out to Stone's Farm in Watertown, book no doubt in hand, to walk in the woods, communing with nature. The name was too prosaic, however, and the spot came to be called "Sweet Auburn" after Oliver Goldsmith's 1770 poem, "The Deserted Village." The first line reads "Sweet Auburn! Loveliest village of the plain." By the time two Unitarians – Jacob Bigelow, a physician, and U.S. Supreme Court Justice Joseph Story – founded the nonprofit cemetery association, the name "Auburn" had stuck. The term "cemetery" comes from the Greek, *koimeterion*, meaning "place of sleep" and Mount Auburn became the country's first garden cemetery. It was a departure from early New England burial grounds with markers decorated with grim images and epitaphs such as: "As you are now, so once was I; As I am now, so must you be; Prepare for death and follow me." The new cemetery was the embodiment of the Unitarian's view of death. The end of life was viewed as the culmination of a natural progression, a reuniting with that from whence we came, the union a welcome, not fearful, event. Death presented the opportunity "to mix forever with the elements" William Cullen Bryant wrote in his popular poem, "Thanatopsis."

I am a lifelong Unitarian-Universalist and this was the notion taught a century later in my Sunday School – that we would essentially all be trees someday. When I walk among the flora of Mount Auburn, it is infinitely comforting to see the expression of this belief so beautifully fulfilled.

My denomination has its own version of saints and many of them are buried in Mount Auburn: William Ellery Channing, Henry Wadsworth Longfellow, Dorothea Dix, Amy Lowell, and Hosea Ballou, among others. Ballou's commanding statue, fourteen feet tall overall, is impressive for its size, but when I walk by, it's his face that is most arresting. More than any portrait painted during his long life, 1771–1852, the warm stone suggests what he must have really looked like, his benevolent gaze a testament to his Universalist beliefs.

A more recent saint shares space with one past in the Fuller family plot. R. Buckminster Fuller is only a few verdant steps away from his great aunt Margaret Fuller Ossoli's cenotaph. Margaret Fuller drowned at only age forty in a shipwreck just off Fire Island, New York. She had been returning from Italy with her husband and small son, both of whom also perished. Only the child's body was recovered and his remains are buried here under the lovely bas-relief profile of his mother on the marker inscribed with the words, "By birth a child of New England / By adoption a citizen of Rome /By genius belonging to the world." I knew Margaret Fuller's great nephew Bucky Fuller (1895–1983) from Maine. He was a well-known and much loved figure in Deer Isle, near where he lived on Bear Island in Penobscot Bay. When I pass his distinctive headstone with its carving of a geodesic dome, I see him standing before the large hearth at the Pilgrim's Inn laughing with my parents during the cocktail hour before one of then innkeeper Ellie Pavlov's outstanding dinners. A smaller stone also rests on his gravesite with the inscription "'Call Me Trim Tab' Bucky." A trim tab helps to control a boat or plane. To Bucky, it meant the way we can accomplish great things merely by exerting a small amount of pressure on society's rudder – all of us these miniature trim tabs.

Another voice I hear is the distinctive one of the poet David McCord (1897–1997), a member of my church, King's Chapel. Two of his poems, "Youth" and "Old Age," are inscribed on the back of his stone:

Blessed Lord, what it is to be young:
To be of, to be for, be among –
Be enchanted, enthralled,
Be the caller, the called,
The singer, the song, and the sung.
Blessed Lord, what it is to be old:
Be the teller, and not the told,
Be serene in the wake,
Of a triumph, mistake,
Of life's rainbows with no pots of gold.

Hear him, and see him, always dapper, with that beautiful smile.

I recently learned that Fannie Merritt Farmer (1857–1915) was also a Unitarian and tracked her down – seeking the headstones of people you "know" is one of Mount Auburn's great pleasures. Appropriately, the small rough-hewn boulder marking her grave looks like a mound of something nice to eat from her *Boston Cooking-School Cookbook* and is surrounded by a lush bed of ivy as a garnish. I own several editions of the book. They have seen much use, serving as inspirations in the kitchen and in my own culinary writings.

Eleanor Hodgman Porter (1868–1920) lies in Mount Auburn too, her stone an elegant Corinthian column with a plaque at the base appropriately adorned with a scroll and quill. Known for her popular Pollyanna books – the first, *Pollyanna*, sold a million copies in 1913 the year it came out – I knew her from her earlier Miss Billy series, one of my childhood favorites. Yes, these books may be dated, but they're still worth a read – and Pollyanna's notion of searching for the "glad," not such a bad one these days. Porter's inscription reads simply: "In Memory of Eleanor H. Porter, who by her writings brought sunshine into the lives of millions." Few writers could wish for more, I daresay.

Charles Dana Gibson is here next to his Gibson girl wife, the legendary beauty, Irene Langhorne Gibson. They're not far from Mary Baker Eddy's monument, an architectural gem, like a small Greek temple, next to Halcyon Lake. For years I heard that there was a phone there so visitors to her final resting place could talk to her, and God as well perhaps. There is, of course, no phone and the story probably arose from the fact that at her death in 1910, a phone was installed in Mount Auburn's receiving tomb for the use of the guards protecting her casket from vandalism until it could be moved to the finished gravesite. Isabella Stewart Gardner's classic mausoleum is also by one of the cemetery's lakes, artistically situated across from Auburn Lake, which looks like a kind of secret vernal pool found deep in the woods.

I visit two relatives, cousins of my father's, their plaque near Perella Path and the main entrance, not all that far a walk from their Brattle Street home. One of my favorite dog statues – there are many of these loyal beasts in the cemetery – is nearby keeping watch over a family named "Barnard." And I visit my great-great-grandmother, Nancy Hills Page who died in childbirth in 1868, living long enough to name her fifth child, "Victor." She had been told it wasn't advisable for her to have another child and selected the name as a symbol of her triumph – a short-lived one. According to the record at the cemetery, she was thirty-seven years, two months, and fourteen days old. I visit her spirit. She was at Mount Auburn only for her cremation before interment in Rochester, New Hampshire, in the Page plot there. Yet, I often think of her, and Dr. William Hussey Page, my great-great-grandfather, when I'm in the cemetery. They were members of First Church in Boston. I have one of their oldest child Nina Page's Sunday School books signed to her from the minister, Rufus Ellis. Dr. Page was Oliver Wendell Holmes' assistant before going on to become House Surgeon at Massachusetts General Hospital and serving as a doctor in the Peninsula Campaign and others during the Civil War. Holmes predeceased William, and I imagine my ancestor attending the service here. And those of others in his generation. Did Nancy walk along Mount Auburn's paths with her other children before her death, an outing to get away from their cramped home on Beach Street? The sense of history, personal and shared, pervades Mount Auburn's landscape. Degrees of separation are erased – sharing a moment with Bucky Fuller reaches back to Margaret; Dr. Page's sisters danced at Lincoln's inaugural ball. And so it continues. That good night, which awaits us all, is eternally expressed, ever regenerating in "Sweet Auburn."

White-winged Crossbill. Photo by John Harrison.

Jeff Meshach

The Birds and the "Trees"

I'm not one to frequent cemeteries. I guess many in the world aren't, even if they've not had to bury a loved one. I, unfortunately, had to visit my mother's grave starting at eight years of age, so when my friend John Harrison suggested we go visit a cemetery, I wasn't at all turned on by the idea.

Then John showed me a few pictures. John does not photograph architecture, nor does he photograph old gravestones for their historical significance. He's a wildlife photographer, and I especially took notice when he sent me pictures of raptors nesting on the Mount Auburn Cemetery grounds. These awesome birds have an effect on me like nothing else in this world, so negative feelings were easily set aside for this adventure.

Yep, I couldn't wait to see a Great Horned Owl nest from literally a few feet away, but the first thing that grabbed my attention as we drove through the gate were the glorious trees. Mount Auburn Cemetery is not just a graveyard on a hill with a pretty iron fence surrounding it. It has some of the largest North American trees growing throughout the property, so even though the word "cemetery" tells you it's the final resting place for several thousand humans, this piece of property is full of life.

First the trees, but only because they were on this earth millions of years before the birds. The trunks of some of the many oaks are so massive you just have to go to them, touch them and gaze up at their impressive crowns. I took a dendrology class at West Virginia University, and I consider that class one of the best I took in my college career because I retain much of the knowledge imparted to me by my professor, Dr. Guthrie. To this day I can identify many North American trees, even from a distance, so just passing through the gate put me in a realm I adore being in. There are oaks, elms, maples, pines and my favorite North American tree, the American Beech. That's the tree with such smooth gray bark that one with a pocketknife just can't resist from carving their initials in. I carry one, but of course refrained. Over the years (the cemetery has been in business since 1831), many of those still living have planted exotic trees, probably because they liked a particular species, but the cemetery staff has ID'd and marked these, so I didn't even have to guess at what they were (even though I still did).

One of the more impressive trees I observed was a honey locust. All honey locusts that aren't the variety *inermis* have spikes growing on their branches and trunks – long, dark and very stout spikes. Some have more spikes than others. With all this "protection," you would think even a squirrel would not want to take a chance on climbing one. Because of the fruit the tree bears, not only do squirrels take the chance, they even will build their nests out of honey locust branches full of spikes they nimbly chew off at the base. If this isn't enough to make you think sometimes wildlife seems daft, a pair of Great Horned Owls chose an abandoned squirrel nest, made of locust spikes, to place their nest on!

John H. and I arrived near the nest around 7:20 in the morning. The cemetery grounds crew placed caution tape (how appropriate for so many reasons) at about a forty-foot diameter radiating from the locust, to keep overly enthusiastic photographers from creeping too close to the tree and frightening off the owls. Mom owl was brooding her two large children as I finally got my eyes on the aerie. At first look I could tell she wouldn't be brooding too much longer, for room on the nest was at a premium. Owls do not bring nesting material to their nest. In fact, most owls nest in tree, building or even dirt-bank cavities. After watching the pile of owl on this seemingly poor choice of a nest for a few minutes, I wanted to damn the torpedoes (and there would have been many coming at me from all respects of the word), climb the nest and wrap caution tape around it. If these owlets and their parents survived to the fledging period without getting their eyes poked out, it would be the miracle of all miracles.

Yep, I am a raptor man, but birds in general interest me. Since leaving college I have become quite interested in Sharp-shinned Hawk food (a prod at my song bird friends), the warblers. John H. has taken some incredible pictures of warblers since I've had the privilege of knowing him, and I always marveled at how seemingly close he was when he took them. I was soon to find out his cemetery secret. Just a short walk from the owl nest brought us to three or four Bradford pear trees. They happened to be flowering, but the birds within their branches on this morning made the flowers seem shriveled and odorless. In the span of thirty minutes we saw a Worm-eating Warbler, Black-throated Blue Warbler, Blue-winged Warbler, Northern Parula, Black-and-white Warbler, Nashville Warbler, Yellow-rumped Warbler and an unidentified warbler. This number of species within such a short time period bordered on a "fallout," which is when a weather event makes all the migrating warblers come to the ground because it's too hard to continue traveling. Those who get to experience a fallout don't forget it for the rest of their lives.

In the St. Louis area the Indigo Bunting is a common summer resident. I don't think twice when I see one. My property and surrounding properties are perfect habitat for them, so I see three to five almost every morning on the way to work. Yes, they are strikingly beautiful, but ho-hum for me. When I mundanely said "Oh, there's an Indigo Bunting" to the ten or so birders under and around these Bradford pear trees, the "OH MY GOD" that came from their mouths, in such a well-synchronized manner, gave the jewels in the trees such a start they may never want to come back to Mount Auburn Cemetery. You can probably guess the Indigo Bunting is not so common in the Northeast.

I have no family in the Boston area. The only way I get to come back to Mount Auburn Cemetery is when the company I work for gets hired again by Zoo New England to present an educational bird show at Stone Zoo, in Stoneham, Massachusetts. This is where I met John, because he comes to a couple of shows a week throughout the summer season to photograph my birds. I recently learned we will be back again next year to present our show. I am already looking forward to visiting the same Bradford pears for fleeting glimpses at the warblers, and having John drag my camera and me to the Great Horned Owl nest again. Most of all I am looking forward to seeing, feeling and smelling the beautiful trees, in all of their spring splendor, within the gates of Mount Auburn Cemetery.

Great Crested Flycatcher. Photo by John Harrison.

Jim Renault

Belted Kingfisher

Green Heron

Red-eyed Vireo

Black-and-white Warbler

American Goldfinch, male

Greater Scaup

Orchard Oriole, male

Orchard Oriole, female

Young Raccoon

Great Horned Owl

Elsa Lichman

Mount Auburn Dell   February 22, 2012

The lowering sun spotlights
the sleeping Great Horned Owl,
his barklike breast, patch of white beard,
and the tips of plumicorns.
A half moon hides amidst tall branches.
The female is dead.

Blunt trauma, I am told.
She carried within two hopeful eggs.
The potential for a new brood,
white chicks in the nest, feeding,
branching, fledging,
gone.

I pray to Mom,
"Hold her for a while."
She cradles the large bird in her arms,
holds in her hand the precious eggs.

John Hadidian

The Cemetery as Habitat and Home

What I know about Mount Auburn Cemetery comes to me indirectly from an ongoing flow of images received from one of its most devoted photo documentarians, John Harrison. John's photographs of Mount Auburn wildlife are works of fine art, but often more than that as well. Not infrequently, he accompanies his images with a narrative account of the animal photographed – where it has been seen before, how many young are being cared for, what its favorite haunts are – personalizing the animal as an identifiable member of the Mount Auburn wildlife community. The fox playing with his young, the Yellow Warbler in full song at tree top, or the raccoon mother trying to corral rambunctious kits high in a tree are part of a larger story. The raccoon and fox chapters unfold year-round, while the warbler and many of his kindred are only summer reading. For the migrants who arrive to nest it is likely, even probable, that they have come back to where they nested last year. This knowledge was first gained through the meticulous studies of Song Sparrows that Margaret Morse Nice conducted three-quarters of a century ago in her suburban Columbus, Ohio, neighborhood. Attaching identification bands to resident birds, Nice documented that the same individuals returned year after year to the same places, opening a new chapter in our understanding of bird life. Knowing this, we suddenly could accord a diminutive brown bird with keen memory, considerable navigation skills, and a sense of place that suggested self-awareness. Even before Nice such thoughts had stirred in another keen observer of bird life, Lucy Baxter Coffin. In 1928, Coffin published a note concerning Song Sparrows in which she concluded that the birds on her Indiana farm could be recognized as individuals *simply* on the basis of their song. From her own observations taken over a period of years, Coffin also noted that the same distinctive singers came back to the farm year after year, until they were heard no more. Like others of her time exploring animal behavior, Coffin had to rely on intrinsic skills – her musically trained ear and considerable patience – to be able to infer such conclusions. Today we have sophisticated equipment to record song and sophisticated sampling protocols to make sure data is collected properly. Then, we have other sophisticated machines to analyze information and rigorous statistical procedures to be able to conclude empirically what earlier observers had to grasp intuitively. Numerous studies have now upheld what Coffin concluded by ear – individuality is found in a wide variety of animal species. That it is not yet in some may be more a problem with our ability to measure it in some animals than anything else. It is strange that we possess the proof, but have not yet concluded what to do with it. If animals are individuals, how should we study them? Understand them? Treat them?

Places like Mount Auburn encourage such thinking, since they only accept us as visitors, respectful and reserved, to come into the very quietude that best suits wildlife. Wild animals may quickly become visible when they are not confronting the brash, noisy and dominating nature we take on elsewhere. We have known since at least the time of Gilbert White that the churchyard and cemetery can be sanctuaries for animals as well as resting places for the deceased. To its own wildlife enthusiasts, Mount Auburn has to seem like an oasis standing in stark contrast to the austere urban landscape surrounding it. To the ecologist pondering form and function, Mount Auburn would be a "habitat island," subject to the same evolutionary forces as the landed islands standing in the oceans. This means that Mount Auburn would start with fewer species than larger lands, lose the ones it had more rapidly, and undergo repeated colonization events as new and replacement species found their way to it. Colonizing events would largely depend on the cemetery's proximity to places where other wildlife habitat existed, however sparse – parks, golf courses, vacant lots, and other pockets of urban land – and, importantly, to corridors that would allow travel from place to place. Railroads would be one example and, in the case of Mount Auburn, the Charles River another. The fortunate few wild wanderers who might come to Mount Auburn could find their sanctuary and future there.

It is strange in a society where we count, measure, or catalogue almost everything that we seem to know little about our cemeteries. Some say there are upwards of a half-million while others put the number much lower. The largest is probably Rose Hill in California, at around 1,400 acres, and the smallest would only be measured in feet, tucked away forgotten in the corner of a field perhaps. The value of each to wildlife would begin with a consideration of their plant communities. How a plant community is structured – its species composition – is critical to the wildlife that an area supports. Many cemeteries are largely open expanses of turf without much plant diversity, often baked in summer to a point that seems inhospitable to animal life. But even an expanse of lawn still supports a living community, from the soil microorganisms that thrive along with the underground grass to the herbivorous giants such as grasshoppers that thrive aboveground. Beyond the diversity it holds, how a plant community is structured can also be critical in meeting the needs of wildlife. Our National Cemetery at Arlington covers a bit more than six hundred acres of largely individual trees dotting a significant expanse of maintained turf. Only somewhat smaller, Crown Hill in Indianapolis preserves a large and contiguous block of trees, a forest really. While the number of trees in the two sites might be nearly equal, how they are distributed matters as well. A thousand trees placed to stand individually and a thousand growing together are very different things, both to the landscape ecologist engaged in study as well as to the wild animals engaged in living. The term "forest interior" is used to designate certain species that do not tolerate living in open areas or at the habitat edges so ubiquitous in urban landscapes. Often, the interior species are more rare and sensitive, and as such become objects of conservation interest. Hence, we speak of a "geometry" of the landscape in which the structural diversity, age, and distribution of the plant community drives the variety of wildlife using it. At 170 acres, Mount Auburn is not as big as other cemeteries, but it is densely and almost contiguously treed with interspersed ponds and open spaces to make it of obvious appeal and value to wildlife.

We certainly need such places if we are to maintain some semblance of the natural world within the urban, not to mention combating losses to sprawl. To some, cities are wholly destructive forces acting upon nature in a way that takes and never gives. To others they are a triumph of the human spirit that rises above the intimidating disorder and unpredictability of the natural world, a signal achievement of the human will. Viewed dispassionately, a conurbation is just another type of ecosystem, different in a number of ways from the forest, grassland or oceans we more familiarly think of, but an ecosystem nonetheless. Cities have no more leave to suspend natural law than any place else. We may torture streams and rivers by encasing them in concrete, even tunnel them under the ground, but we cannot suspend the need for water to move through the landscape. Perhaps someday we will be able to engineer a way to do that, but that does not mean it would be a wise thing to do. What if instead we sought to "Design with Nature," as the visionary landscape architect Ian McHarg put it, rather than come at our cities with brute force as the paradigm for development?

We have always had a choice between trying to dominate the natural world and living in harmony with it. Having largely dominated it, we look back on this now and begin to question what we have done. We speak of biophilia as the innate as well as a learned affinity we have for the natural world, and see it increasingly as an important atavistic need to fulfill, as well as a set of pragmatic practices that we can implement. Directly antagonistic to biophilia is anthropocentrism, referring to the belief that humans are special and endowed with a uniqueness that makes us superior to other living things. We have the power to act as if we were, of course, but that does not mean domination is the right or proper path to follow. The idea that we are superior to other living things is largely self-appointed, and one that is better articulated as that we are different from other living things. That we can be sure of, but then so is each of them different, not only as the abstractions we call species but as the realities we call individuals. Anthropocentric thinking is crumbling, barriers are coming down and we have less and less claim to being alone as unique on this planet. What better place to reflect on all this than Mount Auburn, where the living already are not the center of attention and the dead don't care that they are?

Red Foxes. Photos by John Harrison.

Nancy Esposito

Birding in Mount Auburn Cemetery

The setting is paradise
and paradise is a monochrome
on a Saturday morning, the grey
of rain and tombstone finally lightening
to trumpets of bobolinks, bodiless
among the beech leaves as angels. As the dead
in two centuries of these graves.
The watchers page through hymnals
humming acceptable triads, but
this antiphony from tree to tree
this cacophony
is notation so ancient and luminous
the believers must still chant monody.
Only their breathing tunes to a bird's song.
The hush of the dead supplicates
these silhouetted deities. The wide-angle eyes
of the watchers plead before altars
of foliage, fan their prayer books
to the bright festival of oriole
and bunting, like grafted flowers,
preening among white lilacs.
In a country where the jungle drips
its plumage sits the bird of paradise,
carnival and constant
and silent as prayer among heathens. Even a generous

sky cannot lift the orange and blue feathers
of its flower. But its name makes a litany
of illusion, and still we are unsatisfied.
Find a godless city
street, a shop of finches, trusting parrots,
stacked on metal nests, painted as icons
in a peasant's prie-dieu. A solitary keeper
kindly exacts silver for their song, unceasing,
and not a threnody. A species of dove
the watchers call *mourning.*
The slabs flattened over the dead
conceal more snakes than fabled.
Noise slides from the straight lists
of the watchers who now abandon this garden
as darkness fills the dark hollows
of a blindness enduring forever in that place.
On this side of day silence spills its long, slow warble.

Baltimore Oriole. Photo by John Harrison.

John Harrison

Loving Lucy

Within a few years of my first visit to Mount Auburn Cemetery in 2000, I found my own Red-tailed Hawk. As I explored the cemetery more and more, my fascination with this species grew. The exhilaration of their takeoffs and landings enthralled me. Their red tails, brilliant as the sun shone through them as they soared, mesmerized me. Their proud, fierce demeanor as they perched on a limb, head turning left to right, awed me. They were the monarchs of the cemetery.

They were also a constant presence. I would turn a corner and see one on the grass with a squirrel or a mouse. I would be driving and one would career past my window diving for prey. I would pass Washington Tower in the winter and see one – sometimes a pair – perched on the railings, blue sky above. I would even catch them mating on the tower now and then. I would see them land on a snowy branch, wings extended, with the snow exploding around them, the branch rocking from the force of the landing. Such authority, I always thought. Such command. They were a ubiquitous comfort of the Mount Auburn passing scene. There were always things happening at the cemetery. Every day held new adventures, new species, wonderful surprises. But I could count on the Red-tailed Hawks to be an enduring and endearing presence no matter what else was going on.

I discovered that the hawks particularly liked perching on the weeping beech next to the R. H. White mausoleum (yes, the R. H. White of the stores of my youth). That tree became the most important stop on my growing checklist, as I would visit many times a day hoping to see one of the Red-tails among the branches. And I wasn't disappointed. I would see them there often. It was a stop-off point when bringing prey to the nest as the mate was sitting on eggs or after the chicks were born. On top of the beech they would determine if it was safe to continue from there to the nest. Knowing this we could just wait in that area during nesting season and catch many a takeoff with a squirrel or other prey firmly held in a talon. That striking weeping beech was our very own Red-tailed Hawk photo studio. And all of the hours below the tree watching was like a Harvard University course, Red-tailed Hawks 101. We could never have learned as much about this remarkable species sitting in a classroom, though. We had to be out there!

Watching this tree led me to my first momentous Red-tailed Hawk discovery. In early January of 2005 I saw one of them perched, and watched and photographed it enjoying the sunny day. Within a few minutes, it took off, dazzling me as it always did. But this time, instead of winging out of sight, it flew a short distance and landed in a tall tree nearby – tagged a Norway spruce. It disappeared into the foliage but I watched and waited. Soon it flew off and out of sight. This wasn't particularly noteworthy, a hawk landing in a tree, but for some reason my interest was engaged. It seemed that something else was happening here. Compelled to stay, I watched the hawk heading toward the weeping beech some fifteen minutes later with a branch in its beak. This was the first time I had seen this kind of activity. I was expecting the bird to land on the beech. Instead, it flew right by and landed in that Norway spruce again. I walked nearer to the spruce and through my binoculars I caught glimpses of the hawk moving around. Suddenly I knew what I had discovered. By God, I was looking at my first Red-tailed Hawk nest. It was an exciting moment for me. A revelation.

There and then, this hawk became Lucy to me. I had discovered the nest so I felt I had the right to name her – at least to name her for me. Lucy. She was Lucy. I don't remember why. I'm not even sure there was a reason I chose Lucy. It just came to mind. It wasn't because of the *I Love Lucy* show, I don't think. But that was my Lucy up there in the Norway Spruce using that branch to make her nest.

This discovery demanded closer scrutiny of the nest. I spent hours watching the comings and goings and, of course, discovered Lucy's mate, whom I named Ricky, and watched as they got their nest up to snuff. It was a special learning experience. They were relentless in building the structure and from this I learned first-hand the single-minded determination of nest-building birds. It was hard work breaking branches from trees and bringing them to the nest, but they had a wonderful work ethic. I would often see them tearing branches from a tree. When they broke a branch, the crack was like a gunshot. Sometimes the branch was too strong to snap off and they would pull hard, their wings opening for balance. When they realized the branch wasn't going to break off, they would jump to another branch and try again. It was thrilling to watch. They persevered. They needed a safe, stable home for the young Red-tailed Hawks they would soon bring into the world.

Finding this nest opened a new world to me. I was able to study the activities of these birds day by day. I would watch one of them fly into the nest with a branch and then fly out a few minutes later in search of another branch. Sometimes they would fly into and out of the nest from the same direction. At other times they would approach from one side of the tree and then fly out from the other. I finally figured out that it was the wind that governed the direction of their takeoffs and landings. One day while watching their activities, I saw Lucy fly into the nest from the front and then leave from the rear. After watching her do this twice, I stationed myself below the nest from the rear. Sure enough she soon flew into the nest with a branch from the front, arranged it as she wanted, and then flew out just as I expected. I was waiting for her and captured one of my favorite moments as she leapt out of the nest and flew right over me. It was a breathtaking moment. I was figuring them out.

Lucy taking off from nest. Photo by John Harrison.

A month or so later, on a cold, sunny February afternoon, maybe eight or ten people were gathered near the weeping beech. Lucy and Ricky had made several stops at the tree in the last couple of hours and we were enjoying the show. Suddenly we saw Lucy approaching from the left with a big spruce branch in her talon. She landed carefully on the beech, one talon gripping the branch at the top of the beech and the other talon holding that long spruce branch. Once she landed, Lucy began moving in a manner that suggested she was trying to get a better grip on the big spruce branch which was almost twice her length. All of us watching from below were willing her to take off with that branch. After a minute or so it seemed that she had the grip she wanted and we waited for her to take off. As if on cue, she did. She lifted straight up, her profile facing left, hovered in the air for a brief moment, and then, like a harrier, turned 180 degrees in mid-air toward the Norway spruce and made the short flight to the nest. The snapping of shutters around me as she took off was a symphony. There were ooh's and ah's as Lucy continued the short flight to the nest. Our hopes had been perfectly realized. It was even better than we had imagined. That moment, the long branch in her talon, cobalt blue sky above, eye looking down at us, symbolizes my relationship with this magnificent species.

Lucy takes off from Weeping Beech. Photo by John Harrison.

I have taken thousands of photographs of Sweet Auburn's Red-tailed Hawks since that February day. Lucy and Ricky had one chick that year, Little Ricky. And a couple of years later, when Lucy was no longer there, Hamlet and Ophelia built their nest and have been successful year after year, carrying on Lucy and Ricky's tradition. But this moment frozen in time, Lucy with a branch almost twice as long as her body, lifting off from that weeping beech, looking down at us and turning around in mid-air, will always represent this species to me. Their majesty and their magic. And this moment, too, will always symbolize what Mount Auburn Cemetery has meant to me through the years: A place of wonder. A place of discovery.

In memory of Benjamin and Rose Harrison.

Lucy

By John Harrison

After Lucy

By John Harrison

Peter Alden

Mount Auburn or Bust

Non-birders are often puzzled by the magnetic attraction this botanical oasis has for the ornithophiles of greater Boston. In late April and much of May area birders study the weather charts and try to think like a migratory songbird. Our "Neotropical Songbird Migrants" are a suite of mainly insectivorous birds that winter in the New World tropics. They return to the seasonal abundance of insects and spiders feeding on our summertime leaves, flowers, fruit or each other. Most migrate at night over a broad front whenever they get a following wind (in our case from the southwest).

At dawn these loose flocks search for a wooded area with water and a chance to refuel, have a drink and a daytime snooze (think of a highway gas, restaurant and motel complex). Those waking up over the Boston area see vast expanses of buildings, roads, parking lots and houses that just won't do for an overday layover. Milling around in the sky many note a wooded hill with lots of trees, flowering shrubs and ponds. Migrants arriving over these urban areas will concentrate at Mount Auburn in much greater numbers and variety than in a similar sized area in outer suburban and rural towns.

Not only will you see dozens of warblers and other colorful songbirds on select late spring mornings, you will also find a rare concentration of birdwatchers, sometimes hundreds. A stage of competitive birding we often undergo is to try to see over one hundred kinds of birds in one day (called a century run). A standard route was to do some owling in your hometown, visit Mount Auburn, then spend most of the rest of the day in the Newburyport/Plum Island area. I did this several times with various early birders from Concord and Wellesley with a dad driving. As a high school student and with a massive "fallout" expected the next morning, I would sometimes take the earliest train in, walk to Mount Auburn from the Porter Square stop, and return on another train and walk to the high school a few hours late with some lame excuse.

My father, John Alden, birded as a youth in Newton, MA, and New Hampshire. Most birders go crazy trying to see a rarity or a life bird for their memory and list. My father in later life had no interest in lost waifs, but had warm feelings when seeing again an avian friend from his earlier years. This caused a problem one May morning here when he was trying to show a fine black and orange male American Redstart to my step-mother Anna. A nearby crowd of birders was trying to re-locate a much rarer Cerulean Warbler. My dad re-found his redstart and yelled out "There IT is" to Anna. Before she could get over to see the redstart, dozens of birders had run over to surround my dad asking where IT was.

Pointing out the redstart to all, he witnessed some sneers and mumbles, and learned that the word IT is reserved for the rarity of the day, NOT the prettiest bird to you.

Amongst hundreds of famous Bostonians, Mary Baker Eddy is buried here. Her Christian Science religion eschewed the science of 1800s medicine in favor of prayer. On pointing out her memorial to a singles bird walk crowd I lead most Mays, someone asked who Ms. Eddy was. Trying to point out a singing male Baltimore Oriole I blurted a brief "She was the founder of the world's first free HMO." Prayer is part of healing and it is of interest that one can look out from the top of Mount Auburn and see her "Mother Church" surrounded by some of the world's top hospitals and cutting-edge medical research facilities.

There are dozens of "big names" in ornithology and the bird world present here. Over by Willow Pond lies the granite marker for the untimely early passing of Richard Forster of Wellesley in the 1990s. He worked beside me at Mass Audubon for many years and co-led early birding trips with me to Australia, Spain, South America and Central America. He was a hardcore Red Sox fan. I was with him returning from a Block Island weekend when Bucky F. Dent hit that homer. When "we all" finally won the World Series in 2004, I inked a message to him on a white Red Sox jersey and drove to Mount Auburn and placed it at his site. Why I was drawn to do this is spooky, but I was not alone. I saw Red Sox items at grave sites all over the cemetery. The same was true all over New England as we wanted to share the news with those that departed early.

Mount Auburn, at its best in May, is a recurring annual Woodstock with music by the birds flanked by a rainbow of flowers where souls from the past and present mingle.

American Redstart. Photo by John Harrison.

David Pallin

Painted Lady Butterfly

Young Raccoons

American Goldfinch, male

Great Blue Heron

Great Horned Owlets

Great Horned Owlets

Leslie Wheeler

Mount Auburn Cemetery:
Three Beginnings and an Ending

I first visited Mount Auburn Cemetery at the beginning of a new chapter in my life. Divorced and recently arrived in Cambridge, I was eager to make friends, get to know my surroundings. So when a new friend suggested a visit to Mount Auburn Cemetery, I readily agreed, not only because Mount Auburn was a local attraction, but also because I was and still am fascinated by cemeteries. On a trip to Europe several years earlier, my former husband and I had spent two full days exploring Père Lachaise in Paris, which I later discovered was the inspiration for Mount Auburn. Thereafter, my former and I had made a point of seeking out cemeteries in the various towns we passed through on our travels.

My new friend and I visited Mount Auburn on a glorious sunny day in early fall. The leaves had just begun to turn, and there was a delightful mellowness in the air. The map we picked up at the office included a list of the famous people buried at the cemetery, and I was struck by how many there were. Knowing it would be impossible to visit all the graves, I checked several that I, as a historian specializing in mid-nineteenth-century America, especially wanted to see. Oliver Wendell Holmes, Winslow Homer, Julia Ward Howe, Harriet Jacobs, Henry Wadsworth

Longfellow: these were some of the graves we visited. Some were plain with only the name and dates on the stone. Others were more elaborate. I was particularly taken by Margaret Fuller's grave: a vision of sparkling white marble with Fuller's angular, intelligent face shown in profile, followed by a lengthy tribute not only to Fuller herself, but to her Italian husband, the Marquis Ossoli, and their two-year-old son who "passed from this life together by shipwreck." And, of course I was duly impressed by the graceful neoclassical columns of the Mary Baker Eddy memorial overlooking Halcyon Lake with its shimmering fountain.

But if it was a day of communing with dead heroes, it was also a day filled with natural beauty. Towering trees drew our eyes upward, while bursts of color at ground level brought them down to admire blue hydrangea or pink-fringed hosta, or to watch the ever-changing play of light and shadow on marble, granite and brownstone monuments and blue-green ponds. Steep hills offered dazzling vistas before descending into secluded hollows with "secret gardens." One minute found us deep in untamed woods; the next, in an open landscape of manicured lawns and artfully arranged plantings.

It was a day of stillness, broken only by the distant drone of an airplane, the piping of a jay, the screech of a hawk, the muted sound of human voices. A day of discovery. A day of peace. A day of promise.

Fast forward several years, and I'd begun another chapter in my life: remarried with my first and only child, a baby boy, whom my new husband and I adopted at birth. I pushed him in his stroller all over the city: to Harvard Square and back, around the Fresh Pond Reservoir and the recently created Danehy Park. Pondering where to take him one overcast afternoon in early spring, I decided on Mount Auburn. It wasn't far from where we now lived, and it was lovely and quiet if he chose to nap, which as a mother longing for a break, I hoped he would. And lo and behold, he did! The peacefulness of the place had obviously worked its magic on him. But not for long – or rather not long enough. As we made our way along a winding path, he suddenly awoke and began to howl. And to my horror, he wouldn't stop! Did I forget to bring an afternoon snack that day? I don't remember. All I know is that the only way to get a respite from his crying was to take him out of the stroller and hold him in my arms. He was a big baby, and it wasn't easy holding him and pushing the empty stroller at the same time. At the rate we were going, we would never get out of the cemetery, never get home – wherever home was. Mapless and directionally challenged, I was no longer sure. Like Charlie on the MTA in the old Kingston Trio song, we were doomed to wander the byways of Mount Auburn forever, the mother and child who'd never return.

That afternoon at Mount Auburn was the first of many times my son and I would be lost together, in the car as well as on foot, and once on cross-country skis in the midst of snowy woods and gathering darkness. Finally, after one especially bad experience, he bought me a GPS.

Somehow I managed to find the way out of Mount Auburn that afternoon. My son and I would come back, I told myself. Come back so I could share my love of the natural world with him. We never did. He learned about plants and animals, not at Mount Auburn, but at other places we visited during his growing up years, shadowed by his father's death when he was thirteen and about to enter high school.

That ending brought me back to Mount Auburn on a crisp fall morning. Alone. To pick up his father's ashes. There was no lingering to enjoy the cemetery that day. I simply collected the box with the ashes and left, surprised that a man over six feet tall was now contained in such a small space, though the container was heavier than I'd expected. Nor had I anticipated how hard it was to be doing this by myself, and wished I'd brought a friend along. I didn't bring our son, because I knew it would be too upsetting for him; he'd already burst into tears when I told him his father had been cremated, his father and I having failed to prepare him for this event.

The ashes remained in their box for nearly two years, while I tried to figure out what to do with them. Ultimately, I scattered them at the home in the country my husband had loved, a rural retreat like Mount Auburn. This act helped me move on with my life, and paved the way for another visit to Mount Auburn, three years after my husband's passing, under very different circumstances.

A man I'd recently begun dating suggested a trip to the cemetery. Although he'd lived in the Boston area much longer than I had, he'd never been to Mount Auburn, and had heard about the lovely gardens and the spectacular views of the city from Washington Tower. The rhododendrons were in full bloom that spring afternoon, and we stopped to take pictures of each other against a stunning backdrop of purplish pink flowers. His picture of me became the wallpaper on his computer; mine of him sits on the bookshelf in my living room.

As we strolled along a path leading to Halcyon Lake, we breathed in the sweet scent of viburnum. We sat on the steps of the Mary Baker Eddy monument, watching children play on the grass, while swans glided across the lake, and a snapping turtle floated lazily just below the surface. Then it was on to Washington Tower. Before we began to climb I confessed my fear of becoming claustrophobic in the narrow, enclosed space of the stairwell, but thankfully, we reached the top without a problem. We sat for a long time, talking quietly and admiring the view of the Boston skyline, the Charles River, and the surrounding towns to the west.

It was another day of discovery. A day of peace. A day that held the promise of a new beginning. A promise that has been fulfilled in the years since.

Robert "Boz" Cogan

Green Heron

Fork-tailed Flycatcher

Baltimore Oriole

Black-throated Blue Warbler

Yellow-rumped Warbler

Green Heron

Red-tailed Hawk

Great Horned Owlets

Camilla H. Fox

Connecting with Coyote in
Mount Auburn Cemetery: Bonds that Last

A few months after founding the national non-profit organization, Project Coyote, in 2008, I received a propitious call from John Harrison of Medford, Massachusetts. John knew of Project Coyote and me through a mutual colleague, John Hadidian, Director of Urban Wildlife, the Humane Society of the United States.

I was delighted when Harrison said that he had learned of a coyote family living in Mount Auburn Cemetery. He was making a photo documentary of the animals and offered to share his images. Later that day I received several dozen emails with some of the most stunning images I had seen of coyotes. John explained how he woke at the crack of dawn and ventured out into the cemetery where he consistently spotted an adult family of two coyotes and their pack of seven pups. Perhaps most thrilling about John's phone call was that he and fellow photographers had discovered the coyote family at a time when the pups were very young, so that they would remain in the area of the den site as they were weaned and taught by their parents about life as a coyote on the urban fringe. For the next year John was able to watch these amazing animals from a distance and to document their antics and growth from blue-eyed puppies to full grown adults.

John and I thus formed a bi-coastal email friendship through our deep appreciation of America's Song Dog. We finally had a chance to meet a year later when John came to an urban coyote session that I organized at UMass Amherst. Using his exquisite photographs taken at Mount Auburn Cemetery, John has shared the fascinating world of *Canis latrans* (Latin for "barking dog") a close relative of both wolves and domestic dogs. His images have graced Project Coyote's publications and website and have helped us show the world the wonder, complexity, and beauty of the coyote, thus helping us further our mission of fostering appreciation and respect for America's native Song Dog and other wild canids. They've also helped us to show how places like Mount Auburn Cemetery can set a model for harmonious coexistence with wildlife – even in the middle of heavily human populated areas.

Two of John's photos in particular have garnered an emotional outpouring from many Project Coyote supporters: one of a group of seven pups frolicking in spring flowers near their den and another of the majestic Big Caesar – as aptly nicknamed by John – standing on a hillside covered in snow with Washington Tower above. These images convey the ethos of Mount Auburn Cemetery: that living in harmony with our wild neighbors is of paramount importance in an increasingly fragmented urbanized world. They also show the complexity and richness of the coyote's world – one that bridges both wild and humanized landscapes and the nuances in between.

North America's Native Song Dog

When Europeans arrived in North America in the early 1600s, there were approximately 250,000 wolves living in what are now the lower forty-eight states. Today, about five thousand wild wolves remain. Hunted nearly to extinction, the species was not able to adapt to persecution and the expansion of human settlements.

The experience of America's iconic native "Song Dog" – the coyote – has been quite different. Despite more than 150 years of persecution similar to that experienced by wolves, coyotes have expanded their range threefold since the 1850s and now inhabit all of the Canadian provinces and every state except Hawaii. With the near eradication of wolves, coyotes have found a new ecological niche. Coyotes have adapted to living close to people and can be found in even the most urbanized places, including Chicago, Los Angeles, and New York. But the coyote's knack for coexistence isn't always shared by humans. For while coyotes have little trouble living in human-dominated areas, some people have little tolerance for coyotes.

Big Caesar's family. Photo by John Harrison.

At least nineteen subspecies of coyotes roam North and Central America. As the top carnivore in some environments, coyotes may function as "keystone predators," helping regulate the number and density of smaller mesocarnivores (skunks, raccoons, foxes, feral cats). In this way, coyotes help maintain healthy ecosystems and local biodiversity. Like wolves, coyotes often live in organized social packs, even in urban areas. They also live as solitary individuals or in monogamous pairs.

Reproduction is generally limited to the pack's leaders, the dominant male and female; other females in the group remain behaviorally sterile. Breeding season peaks in mid-February, followed by the birth of four to eight pups in April or May. Males and females may disperse in late fall, and those who remain with their parents form the basis of the pack. In rural habitats coyotes are diurnal, hunting by day and night. In urban areas, coyotes appear to be more nocturnal but can be seen during daylight, especially at dawn and dusk. They are commonly heard howling and yipping at night in response to sirens and other loud noises. With approximately a dozen different vocalizations, two communicating coyotes can often be mistaken for a large pack. Opportunistic omnivores, coyotes take advantage of whatever foods are easiest to obtain: rodents, rabbits, deer, insects, reptiles, and fruit. As scavengers, they provide a beneficial service by keeping ecosystems clean of carrion. Coyotes will take advantage of any accessible food, including garbage, pet food – and the occasional house cat.

I founded Project Coyote with the aim of fostering a new approach in the way coyotes and other predators are viewed and "managed." We are a coalition of wildlife scientists and educators providing a voice for native carnivores, in wildlife management policy and practice, while promoting compassionate conservation and coexistence. We champion progressive management policies that reduce human-predator conflict, support and contribute to innovative scientific research, and help foster respect for and understanding of North America's native Song Dog. We also foster collaboration with other organizations, agencies, and institutions with the goal of promoting active coexistence between people, coyotes, and other native carnivores and reducing the number of coyotes killed nationwide.

Listening to Coyote

As an American icon that has endured centuries of persecution, coyotes have much to teach us about adaptability and resilience. Indigenous tribes revered the coyote for her keen intelligence, mischievous nature, and aptitude for observational learning. The Aztec name for the coyote was *coyotl*, which loosely translates to "trickster," while Navajo sheep and goat herders referred to the coyote as "God's dog." Love them or not, coyotes are here to stay. In the face of rapid environmental and cultural change in an increasingly fragmented world, we could learn a great deal from the coyote – if we would only stop, observe, and listen. Mount Auburn Cemetery offers such a sanctuary for deep listening and communion with nature. And John Harrison is providing the opportunity for us all to touch this magic through his images and words even if we don't have the opportunity to visit this wildlife haven ourselves.

Big Caesar below Washington Tower. Photo by John Harrison.

Big Caesar and His Clan

By John Harrison

Big Caesar's Pups

By John Harrison

Ray Daniel

The Lists of Mount Auburn

"Mary? Mary, do you need a Canada Warbler?"

The warbler-offerer, a woman wearing a fly-fishing hat and long multi-pocketed jacket, waved at another woman, presumably Mary, who had been gazing into the top of a tree through binoculars. Mary agreed that she did indeed a Canada Warbler and joined a circle of binoculared birders standing around a bush in Mount Auburn Cemetery.

"He's in there," said a guy in a Red Sox hat. "He comes out, flies around and goes back."

Mary settled into waiting for her warbler so she could check it off her list, while I continued my walk through Mount Auburn determined to check Charles Bullfinch off mine. For whether it's a checklist of birds, historical graves, sculptures, or trees, Mount Auburn Cemetery inspires the creation of checklists. This makes Mount Auburn an exercise ground for the living in addition to being a sleeping place for the dead.

The checklists of Mount Auburn suggest that lists, and their fulfillment, are concrete expressions of a life well-lived, and that it doesn't matter so much what was on the checklist – "See a warbler," "Visit Bullfinch's grave," "Found a religion" (Mary Baker Eddy) – as it does that we have a list and work on it.

Many gravestones in Mount Auburn connote impressive checklists. They include Longfellow's, a poet whose list included "Write 'Paul Revere's Ride'"; Charles Sumner's, a senator who checked off "Free the slaves"; and Charles Hayden's, a banker who listed "Start two planetariums."

Other gravestones suggest ordinary checklists. They include "Mother" whose list must have included "Kiss a boo boo"; John Brown, a merchant who sadly checked off "Catch a ride on the steamer *Lexington*" (which sank); and a golden retriever designated M.P.S. who lived six years and whose list must have included "sniffing things" and "scarfing table scraps."

Mount Auburn Cemetery itself sits on Boston's List of Firsts, which includes the first public school, the first lending library, the first subway, and, in Mount Auburn, the first landscaped cemetery; indeed it is one of the first places called a "cemetery." Before Mount Auburn's time we had piled our dead into "burying grounds" such as the Granary Burying Ground on Tremont Street.

In providing Boston's citizens with a cemetery in 1831, Mount Auburn's founders provided the first large-scale green space designed for the public. Its establishment heralded the explosion of growth and innovation that distinguished the Hub in the last half of the nineteenth century and built the foundation for a civic pride that permeates Boston and Cambridge today.

I meander the paths of Mount Auburn, and eventually, find myself standing before a concrete tower at the top of a hill. How did I get here? I have no idea. Sometime in my walk, perhaps when I had stopped to take a picture of a fire azalea next to a pond, I had given up on my list-driven grave-search and shifted to a moment-to-moment enjoyment of the gardens around me.

Life can't be all about checklists. Sometimes life has to be about the moment, about enjoying the flower, the tree, the way the sun dapples through the leaves and falls upon a time-melted marble statue. Sometimes you follow the path before you, take your turns randomly, slip into a happy aimless reverie.

Yet now Washington Tower stands before me, inviting me to the top. In the tower's base I find an open door. Granite steps spiral up into the darkness; above me I hear the voices of those who have gone before. I start up the tower. My breath shortens as I climb the unending spiral through darkness towards the light.

I reach the top and join the other tower climbers. We stand against a railing on a small circle of stone and gaze over the curving paths of a garden carefully conceived to elicit reverie and inspiration in equal doses. Beyond the garden we see Cambridge and Boston, cities built and shaped by those buried below us.

The dead sleep through it all, yet, I imagine them waiting for us as we sight a warbler (check), visit a grave (check), publish a novel (check), raise a family (check), climb a tower (check), and, once in a while, stop to savor a moment.

Canada Warbler. Photo by Kim Nagy.

Neil A. O'Hara

Birds Among the Bodies

To birders like me, spring and fall are prime time, the seasons when migration north and south offers fleeting glimpses of the many bird species for which Boston's climate is uncongenial for either permanent residence or breeding. Even species that do breed here – the gaudy orange and black Baltimore Oriole or the more discreet Eastern Phoebe, for example – pass through in greater numbers on their way to and from preferred nesting sites farther north. But the stars of the show, for me at least, are the tiny wood warblers, whose melodious songs resound from the treetops in May as if to say, "Look at me; I'm so pretty in my bright breeding plumage."

Like most songbirds, wood warblers do their long-distance flying at night, stopping at first light to rest up and feed before the next leg of their journey. In open country the birds have no trouble finding suitable daytime habitat, but if they happen to fly over a city at dawn, the patches of green among the concrete and asphalt offer the only refuge. Parks and cemeteries trap the migrants – albeit briefly – and wood warblers over Boston find nowhere more palatable than Mount Auburn Cemetery.

Wherever unusual birds congregate, birders will follow. From late April all through May, Mount Auburn attracts hordes of *homo birdwatcheris*, a species easily identified by the binoculars dangling from its neck. A common subspecies totes a camera; a handful use a spotting scope mounted on a tripod – an obvious field mark for this rarity, although not diagnostic: some photographers mount their cameras on tripods, too.

We birders pay little attention to the great and gifted buried at Mount Auburn. Longfellow's tomb on Indian Ridge is no more than a reference point for the huge deciduous trees nearby, which bud, bloom, leaf out – and draw warblers by the score. The telltale *zee-zee-zee-zoo-zee* of the Black-throated Green Warbler, the insistent rising *beer-beer-beer-beer-BEEEER* of the Black-throated Blue Warbler or the *pleased-pleased-pleased-to-meet-ya* of the Chestnut-sided Warbler draw our eyes upward to the canopy. If we do look down, it is to the north side of Indian Ridge behind Longfellow where low shrubs and dense ground cover provide shelter for the secretive Ovenbird or the bespectacled Swainson's Thrush.

On a typical spring visit to Mount Auburn, I dawdle along Indian Ridge – for an hour or two if the joint is jumping – and then double back around Auburn Lake, better known to birders as the "Spectacles." The water draws Mallards, Canada Geese and the occasional Great Blue Heron; Red-winged Blackbirds cling to the reeds and Common Grackles squawk from above in the trees. I gravitate toward the northwestern "lens," where Yellow-rumped Warblers sometimes perch on the shrubs looking for worms or dart out to seize insects in mid-air. Common Yellowthroats may lurk here, too; they prefer low bushes near water and the males announce their presence with a slow *witchety-witchety-witchety*.

Oxalis Path climbs up the south side away from the lake where careful scrutiny of the steep bank may reveal a Hermit Thrush, a Veery or a Wilson's Warbler, a brilliant yellow bird whose black cap resembles a monk's tonsure. A short walk across Willow Avenue leads to Alder Path, where grass and low cover attract Palm Warblers, which forage on the ground. The gully offers shelter from the wind, too, which brings in Nashville Warblers, Northern Parulas and others on blustery days.

My next stop is usually the Dell, a shady grotto surrounding a small circular pond. At the height of migration, this is often ground zero, and not just for warblers, which come down to drink or bathe, particularly in the late afternoon. A survey of the shoreline may reveal a well-camouflaged Northern Waterthrush, which bobs its tail as it walks, flipping over leaves to find food. The shrubs all over the precipitous west and south sides draw Gray Catbirds and Eastern Towhees as well as thrushes and Ovenbirds. In the trees above, best viewed from Sumac Path or Laurel Avenue, so many warblers flit about at times it is hard to keep track of them all. Rarer species like Bay-breasted or Blackburnian Warblers may show up, not to mention a spectacular Scarlet Tanager (in breeding plumage, the male makes a Northern Cardinal look drab) or Indigo Bunting.

For diehard birders, colorful appearance is a bonus; we delight in a White-crowned Sparrow, an Eastern Wood Pewee or a Least Flycatcher as much as a Rose-breasted Grosbeak. Drab birds often pose a greater challenge – proficient birders still find it hard to distinguish between Least, Willow, Alder and Acadian Flycatchers unless they sing, and during migration they usually don't. Even in the Dell.

Birding is a bit like fishing: you never know what you are going to catch – or where. If the Dell is quiet – or I can tear myself away – I head to Willow Pond. The terrain is quite different; the pond, which is at least four times larger than the Dell, lies amid gentle grassy slopes featuring the occasional massive willow except for one corner lined with smaller trees, shrubs and a few reeds. Not prime warbler habitat, except for Yellow Warblers, which do come and sing: *sweet-sweet-sweet little-more-sweet*. But Green Herons like it, and Belted Kingfishers may turn up as well.

By this time the day is wearing on and I start back toward the main entrance, though never by the shortest route. A hedgerow along Spelman Road beckons. Sparrows and Gray Catbirds hide there, and sometimes the unexpected – a Black-throated Blue Warbler popped out for me once. Then up to the tower, where the trees attract more warblers, or perhaps an Indigo Bunting, Baltimore Oriole or Great Crested Flycatcher. If time permits, another look in the Dell to see what's up and then over to Fountain Avenue for a final check on the thrush habitat below Indian Ridge.

The flowers? Well, they're gorgeous, of course, even if I can hardly tell an azalea from a rhododendron. What's that? Standing on Edwin Booth's grave? Oh, sorry – but look at that Cape May Warbler.

Cape May Warbler, Cedar Ave. Spring Migration, May 7, 2015.
Photo by John Harrison.

Douglas E. Chickering

Birds and Stones

I have a birding friend, Leo, who has a theory as to why Mount Auburn Cemetery is such a birding hot spot. He claims that traces of the spirits of the departed remain in these transcendental, garden cemeteries and this attracts the birds and that the birds and spirits communicate one with the other in a special harmony. Leo is somewhat of a mystic. I have heard much more scientific explanations. Birds migrating at night need a place to come down and the cemetery is a dark place amid all the bright lights of the city, or in daylight, a green oasis among the buildings. It is almost unimportant which version is the most accurate, for the birds do come. They arrive on a fluctuating schedule starting in April and ending sometime in June. Of course there are some birds at Mount Auburn Cemetery year round; but when most people think of the birds of Mount Auburn they are referring to the brilliant creatures of the spring migration. The tanagers, the orioles along with their accompanying cast, and especially the warblers.

Previous to Mount Auburn there were no cemeteries in New England; there were only burial grounds or graveyards. You can still see them scattered in goodly numbers within the various old towns of Massachusetts. The slate headstones with the grinning images of skeletons and crude angels that bear testimony to a

174

much harsher, frightening view of death among the stern and hardy Puritans. One didn't contemplate paradise but instead feared hell.

The people who created and designed Mount Auburn had a different view of the transition between life and the hereafter than their Puritan predecessors. Although I wasn't involved in the deliberations of Henry Dearborn, Jacob Bigelow and Alexander Wadsworth, I think I can deduce that they envisaged a different type of "sleeping place" than the grim foreboding graveyards that threatened the congregations of the churches they surrounded. It was to be a gentle, rolling place of flowering trees and a myriad of colors and scents. A place of peace and beauty. They accomplished this goal with a singular result. And in this garden would be the markers of the departed: in stone, carved with the symbols of eternity, life and a peaceful death. The stones were to be the human symbols, placed artistically among the beauty of the natural world. And, being stone they represented the durable memory of those interred therein. The stones are stately, beautiful and striking as the markers of history, scattered with famous names and reputations. Of course one of the great ironies is that these durable monuments cannot withstand the ravages of the ages and are slowly decaying away. Some seem fresh and bright while others look tired and faint. The spring renews the flowers; it brings forth the trees in eternal beauty and the birds arrive on schedule while the human markers slowly fade away.

Every spring the migrants arrive to rest and feed before moving on. The birds on the wing are what bring me to Mount Auburn Cemetery. This and the fabulous beauty of the garden.

I have many personal memories of Mount Auburn. There is a large monument bearing only my family name: "Chickering." A relative, I am sure, for all Chickerings in North America are descendants of a Simon Chickering back in England. Simon Chickering never emigrated to America but some of his children and grandchildren did. They survived to spread the family and some were prominent. Jonas Chickering was the builder of the Chickering Piano, a highly regarded instrument in its day. I have friends who have insisted on posing with me in front of the stone on occasion. Yet I don't know which Chickering this is.

Of course there are the memories of birds. The tree with five Cape May Warblers in it. The Hooded Warbler hopping out from a bush, almost at my feet. The Mourning Warbler and the Gray-cheeked Thrush basking in the shade at the same water's edge in different years at the Dell. The Bullock's Oriole I rediscovered in a tree by the tower. The Screech Owl high up in a hole, dozing in the sun. Over all there is the diffuse, general memory of wandering down the roads and pathways listening for song and trying to pick out the birds from the treetops, or chasing rumors of a rarity.

And then, lastly there is the mystery. What cemetery worth its salt doesn't contain a mystery? Somewhere in the middle of the cemetery, I think, there is a large plot that is surrounded by a sturdy, ornate, wrought-iron fence – chest high, well maintained, seemingly freshly painted each year. There is a sign that refers to some Scottish Society or club or something, and there is nothing inside its confines except nicely mowed grass. Who or what is this plot waiting for? It always seemed strange and exotic to me. Such a nice, brooding mystery that I almost don't want to know the answer.

Screech Owl. Photo by John Harrison.

Clare Walker Leslie

A Piece About Mount Auburn Cemetery, September 2011

(Written in my journal while walking the Cemetery grounds.)

> September 14, 2011
> 11:30 AM
> Eighty degrees F., hazy, humid
> blue skies/ a few clouds
> single redtail circling high overhead – then stoops

Today, I went to Mount Auburn to see what was there – no lions, no tigers. Just minutes away from emails and teaching and the sortings of family life, I enter a world so different from where I just was –

> the calming presence of chickadees, robins, a catbird, bumblebee,
> turtle, fall asters, and drone of cicadas

Yes, the continual background hum of traffic, sirens, people buzz. But muffled by the acres of rolling greens that now cool my eyes and refocus my soul. I get out my pen and draw acorns as they bang on the walkway and then continue with drawing the chipmunk fast stuffing bits in its mouth. Beady eyes, it stares at me, and I at it – together for one moment, here, before it dashes off to a life I don't know. For over thirty years, Mount Auburn Cemetery has been my studio, my classroom, my place of learning, my place for regaining spirit.

I have been coming here, since 1977, first with Nancy Claflin who taught me the love of birds and then with family, friends, or alone, getting lost in the mazes of lanes and in the mysterious glades, totally forgetting all time. Early on, I began keeping a nature journal, learning how to be a naturalist by watching, filling pages and pages with field drawings and asking questions and finding that, despite my increasing travels to teach, or with family, this Home Place always taught me the most.

I come, today, for a short time between this and that, knowing every tree and path, nuthatch call, chipmunk hole, and blue jay screech by heart. Yet, always there is something new to be watched and delighted in. Right now, it is the bathing of young robins, sparrows, and a cardinal in the long puddle made by the sprinkler system. I watch, laughing away at how funny they all look – madly splashing and fluffing up, scattering water droplets and sending forth those annoying mites.

My journal drawings of September 14, 1982, 1990, 1995, 2000 all show the same things happening here – summer turning into fall. Fruits now forming on trees with starlings, robins, catbirds eating. Masses of insects hovering about on late-blooming goldenrod. Nuts crashing to hard grounds. Yellow-rumped Warblers scooting in and out. A few early-turning-colored leaves.

Here, in nature, everything changes; nothing changes. This continuum – that makes sense in the natural world – is what grounds me. And it grounds those of us who love being outdoors.

It is in this "laboratory" of Mount Auburn Cemetery that I have learned much of what I know about nature and that has given me the skills, over the years, to travel state after state to teach about observing and drawing the natural world and to write books which include many illustrations and observations inspired by these shady glades – this "sweet auburn" of Oliver Goldsmith's poem here.

When our kids were little, we came and explored every patch and pond. They learned to drive the flat lanes. They brought their boyfriends/lovers/spouse to exhale in the beauty and watch the birds. My parents are buried under an old magnolia and I take great comfort knowing I can find their spot and cry by the marker, when needing solace and reflection. I have birded here in all weathers and seasons. A friend and I now honor the seasonal solstices and equinoxes as years turn on years here. When friends visit, my husband and I bring them here as a "special place to experience."

Although my family and I also live in rural Vermont, the intimacy of Mount Auburn, and it's very urban wilderness, never ceases to fascinate me. Vermont has Big Nature that is broad and spread out. Here, you can get close to hawks, butterflies, turtles, rabbits, turkeys, coyotes, and spring migrants. (Once while I was drawing, a coyote came right up to pass by me and I am sure he/she stopped to see what I was doing.)

Come to Mount Auburn and see for yourself the tracks in the snow, the ice on the ponds, the orioles in the oaks, the herons in the cattails, the thrushes perched on the tombstones, the owls hidden magically in the Dell's dark shadows. Mount Auburn Cemetery is, over and above, a cemetery, a horticultural museum, a place of great historic importance. For me, it is a place where nature and city can meet.

Anneliese Merrigan

Mount Auburn Sojourn

Stand.
And the Stygian shadows,
Conjured by ebony gates,
Obscure your face like spider's web
As you saunter along inside.

Pause.
Just for a moment,
As quick as an effortless breath,
And inhale all that this place has to offer.

Wander.
What is it about this enthralling place
That leads one's consciousness astray,
And lets it drift along the meandering paths,
Lined with the lushest of greenery.

Can you behold them?
The tousled raptors,
That soar through the heavens,
Their feathering of sepia, chestnut, and tawny.

Gaze upon them.
Birds nested in towering branches,
That offer their songs
To those beneath the earth.

Drawing of a Red-tailed Hawk in July 2014,
by Anneliese Merrigan, age 14.

Joe Martinez

The Spotted Salamanders of Consecration Dell

It's a sunny mid-morning day in late April at the Dell pond, the water body at the foot of Mount Auburn that forms the base of Consecration Dell. Of the visitors that walk along Moss Path, the footpath that encircles the pond, most will give a cursory glance at the pond then resume searching the trees and shrubs for the migratory birds known to frequent Consecration Dell at this time of year. Some visitors might take a closer look and perhaps see a painted turtle sunning on a small log or a green frog half submerged in the water along the shoreline.

A few visitors will go down to the pond's edge and look closely into the water. There they might find strange-looking gelatinous blobs, about the size of one's fist, attached to the ends of shrub branches dipping into the water. If they look more closely they will notice tiny black dots evenly spaced throughout the gel. Each of those black dots is a spotted salamander embryo; they, in combination with the gel, form what is called an "egg mass." For the day visitor, those black dots are the only glimpse she or he will ever have of a Mount Auburn Cemetery spotted salamander, known to science as *Ambystoma maculatum*. Which is a shame, as that embryo, with a little luck, will grow into an animal as long as your outstretched hand and covered with distinct yellow spots that are in striking contrast with its slate-colored skin color.

To see adult spotted salamanders, you must go to the cemetery on a late March or early April rainy night, when the temperature has warmed, relatively speaking, to the mid-forties and the ground has become thoroughly damp from the rain and snowmelt. Then the salamanders leave the upland natural burrows and manmade crevices in which they spend most of their lives at the cemetery and move above ground towards the Dell pond. Once there, breeding takes place in the water. If you're lucky, you may observe a congress of numerous males swarming around single females. Even a slow night will provide glimpses of adults in the water swimming up to the surface, limbs held back at their sides as they propel themselves with their undulating body and tail, to take a gulp of air before dropping back down to the leaf litter on the bottom.

I first became acquainted with this particular population during the Massachusetts Herpetological Atlas Project of the 1990s and have been monitoring them ever since. Typically I start visiting the Dell pond each rainy night beginning in late March. I take note of the first adults I see migrating to the pond, signs of courtship, and egg-laying. When possible I take photos of individuals. Each has a unique spot pattern and can be readily identified by it in subsequent years. In late April I count the number of egg masses in the water. In June and July I sometimes catch larvae near the shore with either a net or plastic tray to follow their development. By August the larvae will have metamorphosed and moved onto land. In a few years they will return to the Dell pond as breeding adults in their own right.

Spotted salamanders are the most common species of mole salamanders in Massachusetts. They can be found in rural and suburban areas across the state, even in nearby towns such as Brookline, Newton, and West Roxbury. Given that, what is so special about the Mount Auburn Cemetery population?

For one thing, it's an urban population that's very close to Boston. I like the fact that a half-hour walk or a ten-minute bike ride from Harvard Square gets me to spotted salamander country. On a clear spring night, when the Red Sox are in town, you can see the lights of Fenway Park from the top of Mount Auburn. As far as I know, Mount Auburn Cemetery is the only cemetery within the greater Boston area with spotted salamanders.

And consider this: the spotted salamanders I see at Mount Auburn Cemetery are the direct descendants of the spotted salamanders living in the cemetery at the time of its consecration in 1831. As of 2014, that's an unbroken lineage of 183 years. Given that their life span is about ten years, a lot of salamanders have come and gone over that period.

And there's the intrigue: how have they managed to survive for so long when other wetland amphibians, such as spring peepers, wood frogs, and gray treefrogs, haven't? Even the redback salamander, the most common salamander in Massachusetts, has yet to be found here. The cemetery has undergone many physical changes since 1831 and they have persevered through all of them.

And they're here for the long run; the urban location of the cemetery not only prevents them from dispersing beyond its borders but also prevents any recruitment from neighboring populations. Should this population die out, none will take its place. In my opinion, Mount Auburn Cemetery would be poorer for it.

Finally (I could go on, but I'll stop here), each year is different. One year I found many salamanders covered with leeches. Another year a drought occurred after their breeding was finished and I observed, one night, numerous adults in the water along the eastern shoreline with their heads out of the water staring at the uplands where they wanted to be, but the ground was so dry that they simply couldn't leave the water until a good, heavy rain ensued (it eventually did). Yet another year the Dell pond was so flooded that Moss Path was underwater and I did my egg mass count with the cemetery's rowboat!

Sometimes I'm asked if I ever feel uneasy when alone at night in the middle of a large cemetery. My response is to suggest that the questioner consider the people interred nearby. Just to the north of Consecration Dell is George Angell, founder of the MSPCA. On the west slope is Joseph Worcester, who created a dictionary that competed with Noah Webster's. Then there are two of the premier scientist/naturalists of the nineteenth century: Asa Gray, author of *Gray's Manual*, is but a stone's throw away to the northeast and Louis Agassiz, founder of the Harvard University Museum of Comparative Zoology, is a bit further away to the southwest (let's call it a Roberto Clemente stone's throw). Any spectral presence peering over my shoulder is probably just interested in what I'm looking at.

One thing is for certain, come next spring I'll be there, at night, in the rain, seeing what the new year brings.

Spotted Salamander. Photo by John Harrison.

Shawn Carey

Black-and-white Warbler

Downy Woodpecker feeding chick

Gray Phase Screech Owl

Raccoons

Mourning Warbler

Mourning Warbler

Northern Waterthrush

Northern Waterthrush

Raccoon family

Robin

Wild Turkey

Wood Duck

Paul M. Roberts

Preying in Mount Auburn:
The Cemetery and Raptors

For many, Mount Auburn is a destination. For some, the ultimate one, said with special pride as they will take their place of eternal rest next to generations of loved ones. For others, it is the premiere destination in May when the prevailing winds are from the southwest, especially when a backdoor cold front sweeps over Essex County and inundates the coastal littoral, driving migrating passerines into the heat sink inside Route 128/95 and into one of the premiere garden cemeteries in the hemisphere, Mount Auburn.

The cemetery is also a gathering point. I've met birders from Alaska, Missouri, and West Virginia; from the UK and Germany; and from Central and Latin America in Mount Auburn. More important, it is where I see numbers of friends over the decades. Friends I don't see in similar numbers anywhere else, except possibly when there is a Ross's Gull in Newburyport or a Red-footed Falcon on the Vineyard. It is like an annual twenty-fifth college reunion. On those quiet spring days, it is an opportunity to walk, look and talk with many friends. When the cemetery is alive with almost deafening bird song, those friends become a network that rapidly carries word about the Hooded Warbler or the Fork-tailed Flycatcher.

Personally, Mount Auburn has also been a departure point. In my early birding years it was conveniently on my way to work, a great place to start the day birding in April and May. On one of my first days in Mount Auburn, I saw my first Worm-eating and Cerulean Warblers within minutes of each other. This was before discussions of global warming, when there was still excitement about the recent arrivals of some previously southern species, like Northern Cardinal, Tufted Titmouse, and Northern Mockingbird. I was spoiled. But Mount Auburn became a departure point in another way. As I walked Indian Ridge, or by the tower above the Dell, I began looking above the trees rather than into them. I don't recall resident Red-tailed Hawks at that time. The urban invasion of *Buteo jamaicensis* came later, but from that slight elevation in Mount Auburn (emphasis Mount), I could see an occasional Broad-winged Hawk soaring overhead, working its way north. I saw my first small kettles of Broadwings in the cemetery, pirouetting ever higher in the sky before they glided northeast. I was a new birder with a lot to learn.

Occasionally, people would spot an accipiter soaring low over the canopy, trying to catch breakfast. Had to be a Sharp-shinned Hawk. Almost no Cooper's Hawks were seen in the 70s. If you thought you had seen one, you'd be grilled by skeptics. Almost no one carried cameras in those days to document their sightings. There just weren't many Cooper's in Massachusetts, and very few bred north of our latitude. Ospreys were a cause for excitement because they had almost been extirpated from the state. An eagle-sized fish hawk hovering over Willow or Halcyon Pond was something truly rare and special. But the unmitigated highlight was seeing an adult Peregrine Falcon streaking over the cemetery. In the 70s it was unusual for someone to see more than one or two Peregrines in the course of a normal birding year. By the time I yelled "Peregrine," diverting eyes from Tennessee Warblers and Northern Parulas, the bird was gone. If you weren't already looking up, you missed the show. I started looking up more and more.

In September 1974 I went hawk watching at another famous historical Massachusetts birding locale, Mount Tom in Easthampton, where my wife Julie and I saw 2400 Broad-winged Hawks gliding low across the tower on the summit, a tsunami of hawks like we had never seen! The broadwings were streaming low and slow over us, prompting the birders there to drop their binoculars to get a better view. When the wave had passed, no words were spoken, but the birders broke into spontaneous applause. I didn't know it then, but my life had been changed. I began visiting Mount Auburn less frequently in late April and early May because that was the "peak" of what little we knew about spring hawk migration then, as I explored Wachusett Mountain and Plum Island for hawks.

Mount Auburn was changing too. The "huge" waves of passerines in late April and early May did not seem as large in the 90s and 00s as they had been in the 70s and early 80s. Articles on the decline of Neotropical migrants began appearing. We saw discouraging examples of it everywhere, including Mount Auburn, but as metropolitan Boston grew, tied together by ribbons of concrete and asphalt, the small sea of green that is Mount Auburn continued to attract more than its share of migrating birds and birders. Through generations of walkie talkies, and beepers, and portable (not cell yet) phones, and smart phones with texting and Twitter, the old-fashioned human network communicating what special birds were there continued to function with increasing efficiency.

But the fauna of Mount Auburn changed in positive ways as well. In the last quarter of the twentieth century, the Red-tailed Hawk began moving east in Massachusetts. As the old pastures and fields of a once agricultural commonwealth turned into forest, Red-tails lost breeding and hunting habitat. They began to take advantage of the "Eisenhower National Wildlife Refuge," the accidental refuge created by the construction of a national interstate highway system with extensive rights of way often bisecting those forests. New Red-tail habitat was being created. Red-tails began nesting around the cloverleafs on I-90, and Route 128, and Routes 93 and 95. They moved from the first outer beltway (Route 128) down the interstates into the closer suburbs, where they began nesting in cemeteries and country clubs. As those territories were occupied, it was obvious that the wealth of urban pigeons, gray squirrels, and smaller rodents, including meadow voles and even rats, provided a year-long supply of food generally exceeding what they had enjoyed in the abandoned dairy farms and fields. In fact, the territory was so valuable and food so prolific year round that there was little benefit to migrating. Best to remain all year round so some young aggrandizing Red-tail would not take your territory in your absence. Red-tails wintering from Canada increasingly discovered a year-round population of Red-tails moving even farther into Boston and Cambridge, including Mount Auburn.

Mount Auburn became home to nesting Red-tailed Hawks almost a decade into the twenty-first century. The cemetery seems like nirvana for Red-tails. A sanctuary offering superabundant gray squirrels and eastern chipmunks, "sirloin steak" and "prime rib" for the impressive buteos, and with relatively minimal competition from other predators.

Ironically, as metropolitan Boston continued to stretch its concrete and asphalt tentacles farther north, west and south, other species of wildlife, other predators, were also infiltrating our towns and cities. Most notable were the coyotes, who feed on many of the small mammals that Red-tails do, including rabbits. red fox and almost certainly gray fox increased, and the fierce fisher (aka fisher cat) expanded south into suburban Boston, and almost certainly the cemetery. The wild turkey population, reintroduced into Massachusetts almost fifty years ago, also exploded in nearly every village and town – and Mount Auburn. And there were still some long-time resident predators: Screech Owls and occasionally the spectacular Great Horned Owl. Though these owls have been seen in Mount Auburn over the years, the first confirmed nesting was in 2011.

Despite the increasing competition, life seems idyllic for Red-tails in Mount Auburn. Lush forest, intersected by open spaces, with abundant, seemingly naïve prey. Watching urban Red-tails nest nearby on ledges at the Holyoke Center in Harvard Square and on Alewife Brook Parkway, the Red-tails of Mount Auburn seemed privileged. They live in a truly "gated community." When Hamlet and Ophelia, the cemetery's famous Red-tails, had chicks in 2010, unlike most Red-tails they did not drive off their juveniles, forcing them out into the cold, cruel world in late summer/early fall. The kids instead spent the winter and the following spring and summer in "the preserve." This seemed particularly important during the acorn crash of 2011. The dramatic failure of the acorn crop in 2011 after several years of almost incredible abundance caused a sudden, dramatic decline of gray squirrel, chipmunk and other small rodents in the area. Mount Auburn seemed immune to this acute shortage of acorns and squirrels for some inexplicable reason. A second pair of mystery Red-tails built a nest and attempted to breed in Mount Auburn the next year but failed. The established pair, presumably still Hamlet and Ophelia, failed in 2013 but in 2014 fledged three chicks.

The Red-tails and other predators of small mammals in Mount Auburn do face one serious threat to life in their gated community. When they leave Mount Auburn's fences, they may hunt near large grocery stores, restaurants, construction sites, and other sites of human habitation or commerce where one might find rats. Business establishments and multifamily residences often use traps baited with rodenticides to control local rat populations. Many rodenticides do not cause instantaneous death. Thus, poisoned rats can continue to roam and hunt for some period of time. As the toxins accumulate and degrade their level of activity, they become easier to capture. The predators who take those rats, literally easy pickings, can accumulate significant quantities of the toxins in their systems until they, too, die. Humans killing the best natural predators of the rats they wish to eliminate is sadly ironic. Mount Auburn has not been immune to the consequences of rodenticides ingested outside the cemetery. Red-tails, Great Horned Owl, and red fox and possibly other species have all paid the ultimate price of feeding on rats outside the gates.

Yet Mount Auburn remains a haven for Red-tailed Hawks and those who wish to watch and photograph them. The cemetery provides an uncommon opportunity for visitors to observe nesting, marvel at how the young chicks grow, and see them make their first flights. To watch the naïve but incredibly curious fledglings perch on monuments as they loudly beg food from their parents and then gradually begin pursuing four-footed prey on their own. Mount Auburn is famous for its waves of warblers and other passerines in the spring, but its resident Red-tailed Hawks provide insight and entertainment to visitors year round, and there is always the possibility of seeing some other beautiful raptors and maybe a four-footed predator as well.

Fledglings on gravestones, July 2014. Photo by John Harrison.

Je Anne Strott-Branca

Desert Jewels to Mount Auburn Jewels

As an avid birder for forty-plus-years, discovering Mount Auburn Cemetery has been a joy. I started birding in the 70s in Memphis, Tennessee, while a docent at the Memphis Zoo. In May of 88 we left Memphis in our motor home traveling for three months, heading to the East Coast, then north and across the United States, drove the Alaska Highway from Dawson Creek, British Columbia, to Fairbanks, Alaska, then the West Coast to Nevada. Of course I found many life birds along the way. Once in Las Vegas I joined the local Red Rock Audubon Society and really started birding. Up to that time I was a very casual birder; then I became a birding nut (yes, I have flown across the United States to see just one bird).

A friend told me years ago that I was "the only woman he has ever known who loves to hang out at sewer ponds." I didn't want to tell him I also hang out at cemeteries. As any good birder knows they are both great places to bird. I first found out about Mount Auburn from a retired police officer from Brookline, Massachusetts, who had moved to Las Vegas, Nevada. John Trainor would come to the Henderson Bird Viewing Preserve (where I was working), taking photos and birding. He told me of his friend John "Garp" Harrison who takes photos (beautiful pictures not only of the birds, but also the other wildlife of Mount

Auburn). Before my next visit to Boston John and I exchanged emails and agreed to meet on February 25, 2009, at Story Chapel and, as the saying goes, the rest is history!

My friend Cheryl Amato and I met John, then followed him to see Alexander the Great Horned Owl in the Dell. Once we found the owl I was able to see him in my scope. It is always great to share a close up view of any bird with others, but owls are very special. After that first visit to Mount Auburn Cemetery, we regularly meet up with John for another day of great birding whenever I'm back in Boston. It's always helpful to bird with a local who knows where the birds are. On my trip in April of 2011 we got to see Alexander (Great Horned Owl), Roxanne (his mate) and their two owlets. I also had the pleasure of meeting Bob "the Mayor of Mount Auburn" Stymeist and have a photo taken with him. We also met Winthrop, MA, videographer Ernie Sarro, Jimmy Hynes and Al Parker of the Mount Auburn staff, and photographer Chris Livingston.

On January 23, 2011, John took us to see an Eastern Screech Owl. I hadn't seen one in over twenty years; now thanks to John I've seen both the red and gray phase of the Eastern Screech Owl. For Cheryl it was a life bird (which is the first time you see and identify a bird), the first of many to follow. I enjoy coming to Boston in the winter as the birding is always great. And it reminds me of why I live in the desert!

On my last trip to Mount Auburn, in May of 2013, just as we were leaving we saw an Ovenbird. It was the first one I had seen east of the Mississippi River. I saw my life Ovenbird on May 13, 1989, at Spring Mountain State Park just west of Las Vegas, Nevada.

The environment at Mount Auburn is diverse and has every requirement that a bird would need, as well as the other wildlife present, like the red fox (I also got to see a red fox in 2011, while I was in Australia), coyote (lots of them in the West), woodchuck (it had been many years since I'd seen one), bull frog and spotted and snapping turtles, which indicates how well this habitat is maintained. Mount Auburn is to Massachusetts what Cape May is to New Jersey, a birders paradise. Not only is it great for wildlife because of the horticultural collection, it's rich with history with so many notables at rest. One can spend hours just exploring places like the Dell and Indian Ridge.

I've been to all fifty states at least three times, but haven't gotten a life bird for all of them yet. I still have seventeen states to go. Massachusetts is not one of them, however. I've joined the Brookline Bird Club on many outings, but never one to Mount Auburn. I enjoy having my own personal guide in John. I've only seen forty-seven species at Mount Auburn, so I definitely need to spend more time birding here. I just retired in March of 2014 so next spring I plan on birding the East Coast from Florida to Maine, following the spring migration of birds. I would like to reach seven hundred life birds for North America. Right now I'm over 650 for North America and 1,500 for my world list. No doubt Mount Auburn Cemetery will help me get to my goal.

Ovenbird. Photo by John Harrison.

In memory of our wonderful friend, John L. Trainor, Jr., January 9, 1941-March 25, 2014.

Gayle Lakin

Mount Auburn Cemetery:
A Tale Above and Below the Green Grass

A pessimist believes that the moment you are born "you begin to die." So a trip to the cemetery is an anxious reminder of impending death – a glance at grave markers with shriveled flowers or unadorned and forgotten markers. Optimism enables me to see joy in cemeteries. Each and every grave marker is a story waiting to be imagined or told. Since I was a teenager, I came to Mount Auburn Cemetery to wander, observe nature, read, write, daydream, gather my thoughts and to imagine. But in 2008 my reason for going to Mount Auburn Cemetery expanded to the realm of "the personal visit." I stopped at the information area on a summer day in 2008 to request the location of a recently deceased friend, Geneviève McMillan. I received two color-coded Mount Auburn maps – one zoomed in at plot 9562, grave marker 13 and the other zoomed out to reveal the area of Mount Auburn Cemetery around Willow Pond. The inhabitant of marker 13 at site 9562 epitomizes one of many Cantabrigian spirits – on this side of the pond – contributing to the character of this iconic cemetery! Finding her location required wandering through various paths and lanes with my nose in the map and calling over one of the cemetery workers who happily assisted me.

Zooming that lens out from Mount Auburn Cemetery to the larger nearby Cambridge community, my thoughts take me back to my first encounter with this very dramatic, intelligent, life-affirming woman, Geneviève McMillan (aka Ginou) now eternally resting at Mount Auburn Cemetery. One day a librarian at Radcliffe Library called me to ask if she could give me the telephone number of an art collector who had called the library (where my art was on exhibit). The woman had seen images of my artwork in the *Harvard Gazette*. When the librarian informed her that my exhibit would close in a few days, the caller unleashed a rather dramatic tirade. The librarian repeated the words of the caller which included "incensed" several times; the woman was incensed that the *Gazette* had not posted the announcement of this exhibit earlier so she could have visited the Radcliffe Library to see it, incensed the exhibits were not longer, etc. Truth be told, Ginou was soulful and passionate – not exactly a withering flower and perhaps had just not seen the *Gazette* announcement early enough!

I called (617) 864-#### and Ginou answered, "Ah yes..." in a delightful French accent and so began our friendship. She didn't tell me much about herself in that first conversation except to say that she had a passion for African art and absolutely loved the patterning on my ceramic work and absolutely HAD to see it. Could she? So of course I invited her to come to my apartment on Chauncy Street. She casually mentioned that perhaps I could come to her home first to see her African art collection. So I agreed. Sometimes understatement heightens the delight in creating "the element of surprise" and Ginou was a master at this. "Perhaps you would like to see my African art collection" are words that resonated as I exited her home completely awestruck by what I had seen on that first visit. Her home was right in the heart of Harvard Square – a place where students with backpacks continuously passed right by, a place where students noisily went for late night snacks at the now defunct Tommy's House of Pizza, a place where professors, students and book enthusiasts browsed at the now defunct Starr's Bookstore right across the street. Yet, amidst these Harvard Square institutions was an amazing intentionally nondescript "museum" of African art – that was Geneviève's home. The objects were "alive" because each one had its own history and she knew about them in great detail. The maker and the culture of the maker were as important as "the made."

For those of you living in old homes or renting older apartments, do you ever imagine who the past inhabitants might have been or imagine what happened in the space you temporarily occupy whether it be for a year or fifty years? I wonder if the future inhabitants of Geneviève's home will be made aware of her history or will ever wonder about her building. On the day of my first visit, I followed her explicit directions for getting there as I approached the locale. This included walking just past the Hurst Gallery, looking at her gray nondescript apartment building with a maroon Volvo parked in front. I was to ring a small black buzzer that was barely noticeable. At some point I think the buzzer no longer worked and I would call or yell up at a window at a designated time. I repeated that same walk from my home regularly over the years: I walked down Mass Ave, crossing over Waterhouse Street; passed Out of Town News; looked up at the gold lettering of the *Car Talk* offices – "Dewey, Cheetham and Howe" – and eventually hung a left on Mount Auburn Street from JFK Street; saw the familiar purple, gold, and red paint of the *Harvard Lampoon* and came upon the most unassuming of places – Geneviève's light gray apartment building.

The living quarters were on the top floor with a balcony overlooking the convergence of Mount Auburn and Bow Streets. There was not one area that was free from artwork in her home, yet the works were regularly dusted and well cared for. Even as I would walk up the stairs, I had to navigate around the art. Most of Geneviève's collection was African art, but there were also some pieces by local emerging artists or of iconic artists like Alexander Calder – all had a personal connection and/or a history that had meaning to her. On each visit, she would select a few pieces to talk about over wine, or I would wander around and make my own inquiries. As time passed, she lamented about the great inconvenience of a mind being trapped in a body ravaged by age and would talk about the museum officials coming to her place to photograph her collection for cataloging purposes. Before her death, she bequeathed most of her collection to the Museum of Fine Arts, Boston.

Her story goes well beyond her art collecting: her French upbringing; being a "war bride" and marrying Robert McMillan, one of the founders of the Architects Collaborative (along with Walter Gropius); divorcing her husband and the suburban lifestyle; owning an authentic French dining establishment popular with Harvard University students and faculty called Henri IV; supporting artists (one artist near and dear to her was a painter, Reba Stewart); an enduring friendship with another Harvard Square icon, the original owner of the Café Pamplona; and most importantly her extensive philanthropy that always involved supporting the diversity of people and cultures of the world and making connections.

I was touched that Geneviève wanted to purchase my work. She invited me to her home; came to mine (although she hated the stairs); invited me to the theater and to see films at the Harvard Film Archive; talked about art, philosophy, literature, and politics; and we shared stories about our lives. I always felt her stories were a lot more interesting than mine! I was so taken by the fact that she wanted my work to "live" amidst her collection that I insisted it be a gift. Her response was, "Ah, but Gaël (this is how she pronounced my name), I am a collector and you are an artist." My piece was surrounded by African art on a low table in front of the sliding glass doors that looked out onto that convergence of Bow and Mount Auburn Streets – what a view! It was her passion that was the final spark that made me pursue my own passion more in depth. I was always pursuing art for the simple reason that I love it, but decided to go to graduate school for my MFA. She would call me periodically during those two years and would ask how I was doing and what was happening. If you find or walk by her grave marker, just realize that I was just one (and one of the lesser known) of the many lives she touched. With a bit of research, you will understand the far reaches of the causes she supported!

My reflections on Mount Auburn Cemetery have come full circle as I recall a visit this past August. I visited Ginou's resting place and then wandered to a favorite spot at Auburn Lake where I often see frogs, turtles and blue herons. Before I approached the site, I noticed a parked car with a giant camera lens sticking out from an opened window. I instinctively paused – there surely was something interesting to look at that I did not want to disturb. A man was photographing a group of rabbits feeding on the grass in front of a mausoleum! The car eventually moved along and I proceeded to Auburn Lake. Within minutes I saw a blue heron and down the way noticed the car again with the same man standing near it with camera in hand. I signaled for him to come over and quietly said, "There is a blue heron!" This man responded, "Ah, the heron is back…" – and so began the start of a new friendship with an amazing New England nature photographer, John Harrison! He showed me his recent images of a family of raccoons in the hollow of a tree near Bigelow Chapel and an image of a fox carrying off a squirrel somewhere on the Mount Auburn Cemetery grounds. He continues to share his nature images at Mount Auburn Cemetery and I happily share them with my students.

Shortly after that trip, I returned with my father who is a history buff, but ironically had not spent much time at Mount Auburn Cemetery other than maybe one visit or two. He is elderly and loves walking, but does so with difficulty, so I purchased a CD driving tour of the cemetery and we drove around, stopping at various points to view and hear about the significance of a particular location, a mausoleum, or statue. We eventually got out of the car, sat on a stone bench overlooking a pond, and he reminisced about the graduate student apartments for married couples on Shaler Lane, about Elsie's Sandwich Shop, dates with my mother at the Wursthaus, Jim and Gerry/Cathy and Dick (some of his dear Harvard friends and their spouses) and more about his days in Cambridge. It is one day among many at Mount Auburn Cemetery that I cherish. Later in the summer, I repeated the driving tour with my mother who was delighted by the bird-watching (making note of the bird sightings listed for that week on the chalkboard) and the beautiful plantings. Since that time, my parents have taken many of their friends on that same driving tour. They even managed to be on the lookout for John Harrison and found him by using my description – just look for the professional photographer! They are now friends with him too.

I recently had a conversation with a friend about the death of her father. This conversation is the perfect way to share a final thought about Mount Auburn Cemetery. My friend was visiting her father in the hospital at the time he was facing end of life issues. As she left the room to go home, her father registered the sadness on her face and tried to make her feel better by commenting, "Don't worry, I am still on the same side of the green grass!" When my time comes, I cannot think of a better place to rest when I am "no longer on the same side of the green grass." Mount Auburn Cemetery is far from a "dead" place even if cemeteries "bury the dead"!

Great Blue Heron under bridge at Auburn Lake.
Photo by John Harrison.

Kate Flora

Dead in Good Company

My mother was an amateur genealogist and a big history buff, so as a child I was often dragged to cemeteries so she could read the headstones, take her notes, and encourage us to admire the carvings and the crypts. Cemeteries in our part of Maine tended to be built on hilltops, affording those who wished to visit the dead marvelous vistas that left me with a sense that visiting those spots, and mourning and remembering those who were gone, was an act that should be done in a place where the beauty encouraged return and remembrance. Visiting cemeteries under my mother's wing, and pondering what the headstones had to say, also left me with a deepened interest in history and a lingering curiosity about the stories behind the words.

As a result, I grew up with a sense of cemeteries as fascinating places, places of physical beauty that yielded up the inhabitants' stories in tantalizing little bits. Headstones told of heroic deeds and tragic losses. They told of disease and disaster, of lives cut short, of status and stature in the community and in the nation. Depending on the architectural and design trends of the period when someone died, a grave might bear a compelling statue, an elaborate headstone, a grand mausoleum or the simplest of markers. Each could convey, in its own way, a sense of the person gone. The deceased might be buried alone, or be surrounded by generations of family.

Often, a row of tiny headstones detailed the effects of disease in the same way that the famous six word story – *Baby shoes for sale. Never Used* – does. Sometimes, the headstone would also chronicle more than one wife or husband lost.

In Mount Auburn, among the winding paths and the lovely trees and shrubs, it is easy to be inspired not only by the surroundings, but by the lives of those who lie there. On the headstones and monuments and plaques, the lives of so many who made an impact on our nation are detailed. Inventors and scientists. Inspiring preachers. Civil War and other military generals. Harvard College presidents. Supreme Court justices and other outstanding jurists. Governors, congressmen and senators. Artists and writers and musicians. Great baseball players. Men whose names are still on our lips today, such as the great organist, E. Power Biggs, and the author of the iconic book on familiar quotations, John Bartlett.

You may stroll past Nathaniel Bowditch, the father of modern navigation. James Chickering, of piano fame. The great architect Charles Bulfinch. B. F. Skinner. Civil War hero Robert Gould Shaw (though he is only memorialized; it is thought, though it's not certain, that his remains were taken by the sea). In this company, along with the ways in which visitors are moved by the natural beauty of this great place, there is a genuine sense in the air of achievement and accomplishment, of those who dared, those who wondered, those who aspired and those who dreamed. It is a scent as heady and rich as the trees and flowers and the rich soil that nurture them. This is a place where inspiration can truly be drawn in with every breath.

Because my mother was a feminist, she often focused on the women's headstones, or lack of them, calling my attention to the number of wives who died young in childbirth, or whose data was not deemed worthy of inclusion. Women were often dismissed in the brief phrase, "and Sarah, his wife." And it is true, in this company, that most of the professions or callings that gave these men of distinction their fame were (and in some cases still are) denied to women. But despite the ways in which society denied them opportunities, women game changers are well represented in the stunning company of the dead who rest in the beauty of Mount Auburn.

A woman stroller, seeking inspiration, may not only aspire to those professions formerly the sole province of men, she may find shining examples of women who achieved success, challenged the status quo, and worked for change in the worlds they inhabited. Among them are the Fannys – Fanny Osgood, the poet; Fanny Fern, the newspaper woman whose outrage that Fanny Osgood rested without even the grace of headstone brought both of them further fame and recognition; and Fannie Farmer, champion of exacting measurement and good nutrition, whose iconic cookbook still stands on the bookshelves of millions of households today.

Then there are the reformers – the women who took on the system and challenged its assumptions. Among them Julia Ward Howe, women's rights and anti-slavery activist, who, at her friend James Freeman Clarke's suggestion, wrote new lyrics to "John Brown's Body," which became "The Battle Hymn of the Republic" (Ward was paid $5.00 for it); the inspiring Josephine St. Pierre Ruffin, journalist, suffragette, and early civil rights activist, who fought against slavery, recruited for the Massachusetts 54th Regiment, and founded the country's first newspaper for African-American women; and Dorothea Dix, crusader for humane care of the mentally ill, and supervisor of nursing during the Civil War; and not least, of course, pause before the mausoleum of Mary Baker Eddy, who founded the Christian Science Church.

Breathe in. Breathe out. Inhale the talent of another poet, Amy Lowell. The craft of sculptor Harriet Goodhue Hosmer. Imagine the pleasing tales of Eleanor Porter, author of the Pollyanna series. Envy and be inspired by the scientific acumen and management abilities of Elizabeth Aggasiz, scientist, writer, and president of Radcliffe College. Then let your imagination soar with Isabella Stewart Gardner, art patron, art collector, and grantor of that great gift to the people of Boston and the world, the Gardner Museum.

Some go to Mount Auburn for the flora. Others, armed with keen eyes and cameras, come for the fauna. I go for inspiration. For the great company of the dead, and the possibilities they represent for how life can be lived.

Groundhog. Photo by John Harrison.

Ray Brown

Lost in Sweet Auburn

Anyone who's traveled with me in my car knows about my sense of direction. I don't have one. And nowhere is this more evident than when I visit Mount Auburn Cemetery, long known by the musical and apt sobriquet "Sweet Auburn." Typically, if I have a couple of hours there, I spend the first ninety minutes trying to find birds and the last thirty minutes trying to find my way back to the entrance. On one visit I drove deep into the cemetery instead of parking near the entrance, but avoided repeating the practice after I realized that it's even harder to find a car parked in a forgotten location than to find it out near Mount Auburn Street.

In my defense I'll point out that there are dozens of named streets and paths at Mount Auburn, and even some street signs that seem not to be associated with any kind of thoroughfare at all. That poses quite a challenge for someone who can't find his way to Brookline without consulting a GPS unit.

In fact, I actually tried using my iPhone's GPS to find my way around the cemetery one day, and managed to get even more lost than usual. There's a tricky little section on the west side, where an arm of the property juts out and is separated from the main part of the grounds. I had managed to make my way to that arm,

213

where a masonry wall blocked me from accessing the cemetery proper. I wound up on Grove Street (I think), where I commenced a thirty-minute walk north and east to re-enter the cemetery by the main entrance.

Several times along the way, though, I'd forgotten about being lost when I managed to see my first-ever Blackburnian Warbler in the top of a tall spruce. Many people, upon seeing this spectacularly colorful warbler, might shout out its name, but I could only quietly contemplate that I'd just seen the bird that had gotten Phoebe Snetsinger hooked on birding. Phoebe found her way all around the world, breaking the record for most species (8,398-plus) ever recorded. I was just trying to find my way back to the cemetery entrance. More pleasant distractions followed, including a close-up view of an active Baltimore Oriole's nest – a marvelous pendulum-shaped creation that's typically placed near the end of a thin branch, a location that helps protect it from heavyweight predators trying to access its potentially delicious contents.

Another delightful sighting on this same visit kept me temporarily distracted from my direction-challenged plight, as I watched a Black-and-white Warbler work the branches of a maple tree, probing the bark for insects while I listened to his distinctive "squeaky wheel" song. Finally, like a sailor spotting a flock of birds telling him that land was near, I saw the green line that winds its way through the cemetery and provides a route (assuming one follows it in the right direction) back to the main gate and civilization just beyond.

My most recent Sweet Auburn experiences were indoors. On May 4, 2014, I hosted my Sunday morning *Talkin' Birds* radio show live from another place that helps make Mount Auburn special: the nineteenth-century red sandstone Story Chapel. And, as luck would have it, I returned there just a couple of weeks later, serving as MC for a wonderful program called "On the Wing – A Celebration of Birds in Music and Poetry." Both events were blessed by nice turnouts of bird and music and poetry lovers.

It was easy to find my way out of Mount Auburn from Story Chapel, what with it being just yards from the cemetery's entrance, although I knew I'd probably replicate my wayward wanderings on my next visit. Still, I figured that if I'm going to get lost for half-an-hour (or more), Sweet Auburn is a pretty good place to do it.

Talkin' Birds host Ray Brown (foreground) with (L-R) engineer Ryan Stanton and producer Mark Duffield. Photo by John Harrison.

Wendy Drexler

Heron at Willow Pond

Her legs are a long and silent shear as she
strides, a slow ripple bending low.
Her neck sways like a wave, like branched bur-reeds.

She stands and scans the underwater shadows,
thrusts her neck, opens her bill, clamps down
upon a frog. And why does she dip that bill –

is it to wash the frog in the algal broth
of silt and moldering leaves in which she stands?
Now she shakes her head, a handkerchief fluttering,

then rachets back that squirming, mud-green head
into the cave of her mouth. But the frog flails,
kicks its legs, its belly flashes white,

refusing to surrender, the heron not
yielding, everything at stake when your life
is what you have to lose. And the frog

spills from the heron's bill into the dark
vein of water. Not even a crease on that
pond as the frog swims away.

The day grown old, the heron furls her wings,
shifts from foot to foot, feathers quivering,
and the whole spent world comes rushing back.

Great Blue Heron. Photo by John Harrison.

Andy Provost

Coyote Pup

Coyote

Great Horned Owlet

Red Fox

Coyote Pup

Hooded Merganser

Kim Nagy

The Owls

It seemed misguided and depressing to me, taking my seventy-five year old mother to a cemetery. Was the Companion visiting anyone? I asked. Not that I know of, responded my mother. Apparently they went twice a week, every week. Was it Mount Auburn Cemetery? Mount Auburn Cemetery is America's first landscaped burial ground, and very beautiful, I told her. I don't remember, she said.

Late in 2010, I moved my mother to Boston from New Jersey, completely unprepared for her mental state, precipitous cognitive decline, and excessive neediness. Thus began my "Alice in Wonderland" odyssey down an entirely new rabbit hole. When I discovered Senior Companions for my mother, I hired three very different women to spend a few hours each day with her during the week, affording me greatly appreciated respite.

My mother answered "I don't remember" every time I asked her what she did when she was with the Companions, even if it was just minutes after they left. Through a structure of stability and counseling, my mother improved over time, and one day she announced that she "went to the cemetery all the time" with one of the Companions. I was more surprised that she volunteered the information than by their choice of activity.

In 2010, I experienced unexpected and non-stop losses - an executive job, my mother (figuratively), and some core relationships that I thought would last forever. It seemed all I had left at this point was my love of nature photography. In March 2011, I took my mother to Florida to see her childhood friend. At a bird refuge I met a nature photographer who lived in Massachusetts, and he told me of other local wildlife photographers, whom I contacted when I returned.

After a few social exchanges, John Harrison recommended meeting at the Mount Auburn Cemetery, not only because it is a destination for migratory birds, but also because it is designated as a Massachusetts Important Bird Area. The big news at the time was that Alexander (the Great Horned Owl) was now seen alone, as his mate had left at the end of February, presumably to find a nest and incubate eggs. He showed me where Alexander slept high up in an evergreen, and that was quite a sight to see.

The next time John called, he told me to meet him at the base of a honey locust tree to witness a true miracle – the owl's nest. Alexander's mate, Roxanne, was sitting on two recently hatched owlets. Apparently this was the first such event that anyone could remember, having an owl nest so visible to all. Previous years of owl couplings had sadly ended in failed nests, and even the death of an owl one year. This was a very special occurrence; a great sign. To me it seemed propitious, as owls are my favorite bird.

Then I started going to Mount Auburn Cemetery nearly every day, but not with my mother and her Companion. Watching the growth of the owlets brought me such happiness that I forgot my challenging situation for as long as I was on the grounds. Since the owlets were nocturnal, they were asleep most of the time, and I sat on the grass not so much waiting for them to do something, as just being happy to be near them. I was looking for new tools I needed to rebuild my old self, and watching the owls helped me a lot. They inspired action in me by uplifting my spirit, and they encouraged me to be cheerful merely because of their existence. I used to predicate "feeling happy" on external must-haves, thereby setting up a contingency basis for happiness. This was not a successful long-term strategy.

The owlets were just beginning their lives and I was entering a new phase in mine. In early April, they were covered by their mother Roxanne, struggling to steady their oversized heads on fragile necks, focusing on the new world before their eyes, yawning and wobbling and then drifting off to sleep again. They were transforming quickly, living life forward, making progress every day. I knew that my own personal experience and ultimately how I processed it would provide the final piece for the transformation I too would have to undergo to become the person I was meant to be.

In learning how to deal with my mother as she was now instead of who she used to be, I was learning how to navigate in a new world and, like the owlets, master new life skills without a roadmap. Fear had always played a leading role in my life, but after so much loss, I was forced to master the turbulence, and then I stopped being afraid. The world might seem to be a scary place, but it all depended on interpretation. The owlets and Roxanne were stuffed into a very small nest, surrounded (or protected) by long sharp thorns, exposed for all to see, and not even that high off the ground. Neither Roxanne nor the owlets ever seemed stressed, and after a short time, they appeared to lose interest in all their photographer and birdwatcher fans. Probably we just blended into their background and became part of their landscape.

As the owl family grew, so did their fame, and soon there were many people visiting them, even during the week. The owlets became celebrities; any movement from them or Roxanne set off a series of shutter snaps from the photographers below; a yawn from any of them increased the activity to a near frenzy. My neighbor asked what I did with my time, now that I wasn't working. I cheerily replied: I go to the cemetery! Then I told her about the owls.

Getting a good shot really was a challenge. It was an unusually cold spring after an unusually cold and snowy winter. Sometimes the weather was perfect but the owlets would be sleeping and other times they would be awake and moving a bit, but it would be one of those dreaded "white days." Figuring out the proper exposure was also tricky, but I have always had faith in the transformative power of frustration, and so I kept trying. You learn patience if you want to photograph wildlife. I wondered if the owls had a sense of humor and later picked photographers they liked more than others, telling each other to wake up or go to sleep, depending on who was taking pictures.

Most of the time Roxanne was half asleep on the nest and the big event was when one of the owlets pushed on her feathers, trying to get some air. It was funny to watch the feathers move before the oversized beak and fuzzy head appeared. Once, after sitting on the cold wet grass, I detected some movement in the mother, as opposed to movement from below. I stood up. Was she going to…? Could she just leave the nest? Is she going to fly? I was ready, and when she suddenly leapt off the nest, I got the shot. The two little owlets seemed groggy and confused, not quite registering what had just happened. My favorite part of that photo was the impulsion in her legs, which were strong and fully feathered.

Like my mother and her Companion, I kept going back. Some days I didn't shoot any photos at all. I just enjoyed the owls. When things were very stressful and difficult with my mother and her increasing emotional demands, I spent more time in nature. It was a healthy distraction. As the owlets grew, Roxanne left the nest more often but she always watched from a nearby tree. Alexander fed them well; they grew quickly and were soon branching. When they got older, I showed my mother the nest, and the owls made my mother enjoy Mount Auburn even more.

Then it really got fun. The owlets were very close and affectionate with each other; they were always touching and playing. The older one (by a week) took to craning its head, seemingly curious about the many pairs of binoculars at any given point of the day. The head movements were adorable, as the owlet craned high, swooped down, moved one way and then the other. They were fuzzy and plump, and soon would outgrow the nest.

The last file I have from photographing the owls is called

"owlets – last time on branch," dated late April. John had told me that their departure was imminent, and he was kind enough to call me on that very active Saturday to observe them.

There was a huge crowd that day. Shutters were snapping continually. The older owlet had climbed to a higher branch, alone. They were very large now, but still all fuzzy instead of sleek. On the older owlet, one ear tuft was longer than the other, giving the bird a comical expression. Their eyes were large and golden. The weather was beautiful too, and the honey locust tree had sprouted leaves. I had a feeling that these would be my last photos of them.

I returned to Mount Auburn the next day, wondering if they would still be there. Both of them were very high up in the tree. Their backs were turned to the two photographers who were there; I didn't even bother to take any photos. I just wanted to remember the experience. They were awkward and still couldn't fly proficiently. The younger one was on a weaker branch, and when a gust of wind came, it held on, extended its wings for balance, and rocked comically. The day after that they were gone.

There were sightings of the owlets with Roxanne in nearby trees, and they were always close to Alexander. All the photographers were gone and the nest was empty. The new spring growth began to envelop the nest, and all was quiet. Except for a well-worn path up the hill to the honey locust tree, it was like nothing had ever happened.

I am deeply grateful that I met John, who showed me the owls. It was a wonderful experience, whetting my appetite to seek out similar adventures. Being on the grounds of Mount Auburn Cemetery made me feel closer to who I used to be, and the owls just made me happy. When I reflect on my life, I know that transforming pressure and challenge successfully requires blind faith in a positive outcome. It's nothing short of expecting a platform to materialize as you step over the edge into what appears to be an abyss. Like the owls, when they left the nest for the first time, they would either fall or they would learn to fly.

It is my hope that some morning I will wake up, happy as I

used to be. I've learned that at the bottom of all grief lies a gift, but we have to dig deep for it. We meet the people we need to meet and we have certain experiences when we need them. At the time, we might not know why things happened as they did, but oftentimes later, we do. I hope one day all the sadness and stress of the experience with my mother will be a distant memory, so that when I reflect on her I only remember the gift, just as when I see the empty nest in the honey locust tree in the Mount Auburn Cemetery, I only remember the owls.

Ziggy the Great Horned Owlet. Photo by Kim Nagy.

Kim Nagy

Great Horned Owls

Young Raccoons

Coyote "Lois"

Wild Turkey at Auburn Lake

Northern Parula

Northern Cardinal, female

Bullfrog

Downy Woodpecker, male

Northern Cardinal, male

Hooded Merganser

Coyote "Blondie"

Northern Flicker

Great Horned Owlet

Great Horned Owlet

Palm Warbler

Squirrel

Coyote "Lois"

Maryanne O'Hara

I Always Knew It Was Temporary

My earliest cemetery memories: they are adventurous in the way that kids can make an adventure out of anything. We see who will be the first to spot our grandfather's grave. We choose "three favorite headstones" and fight over who gets the one with the two doves. We gasp over the children's graves. Our mother mourns each one: *Look, the poor little soul. Only two years old.* And we shiver a little.

Later, as a high schooler, I'm part of a group that smugly realizes that if we party in the local cemetery, the cops will never find us. We go out of our way to be mindful of where we are. We are respectful. One night, we notice that a tall, ancient headstone has toppled over and we all pitch in to try and heft it back into place. The stone is surprisingly dense; we fail, and that frightens me in a way I don't understand.

The cemetery is full of these old, weathered stones. The old-fashioned names they bear, like Asaph and Elijah, make the people who possessed those names seem not quite real. Yet they were, they were – because there, on the second path, is a heart-shaped, freshly-cut stone, made for the girl who had been our age when she died just a few years ago. Pretty, gangly, tall, and sweet, with long brown hair parted in the middle, Jean went out of her

239

way to smile and be kind to everyone. I thought she was an angel. There were whispers of leukemia, and then she was gone.

In graduate school, I explore Cambridge, and Mount Auburn becomes a favorite place to walk with my new friend who lives over on Huron Avenue. Mount Auburn is a sanctuary for birds, a horticulturalist's delight, and a history and literary buff's dream. With maps in hand, we seek out all the illustrious names: Longfellow, Homer, Isabella Stewart Gardner. We read "Electra on Azalea Path" and hunt for Otto Plath's grave, and it just seems wrong to realize that he is buried on another Azalea Path, an unmarked one, in Winthrop, Massachusetts. We want to rewrite history the way we write fiction and poetry. The Plaths seem like they belong in Mount Auburn, and Mount Auburn, in turn, feels like a small Mount Olympus, a place where our human Gods live on. Mount Auburn is the kind of leafy, lush place that can almost make you forget that there aren't different kinds of dead.

Later, I write a novel, *Cascade*, which is loosely based on four Massachusetts towns that were flooded in the 1930s to create the reservoir that feeds thirsty Boston to this day. The towns' cemeteries were relocated to a single plot of land, the Quabbin Park Cemetery, a tidy and reverent space that I visit when I research my book, and which disappoints me. I model my fictional town, Cascade, on the four towns, but create a fictional Cascade Park Cemetery that I model on Mount Auburn:

The state had tried its best to make the new cemetery glorious, magnificent. The landscaping was composed of hedges and flowering trees and pebble-stoned paths named Azalea and Gardenia that connected clusters of plots to clusters of plots, each cluster presided over by leafy oaks and maples...

Remembering how hard it was to imagine the real lives of Asaph and Elijah, and how necessary it seemed to remember Jean, I write:

Dez stood over their headstones, situated near a maple sapling on Peony Path. William Aloysius Hart, 1864–1934. Caroline Haywood Hart, 1884–1918. Timon William Hart, 1910–1918. Lives defined and reduced by a bracketing of numbers.

Once someone was dead awhile, it was hard to believe they'd really existed. Dead was dead. Past was past. Yet the processing of the centuries would go on. Desdemona Hart Spaulding, 1908–.

Timon's eight years looked negligible on stone. They were slim digits that in no way conveyed that his eight years had seemed longer because they had also seemed endless. Timon's skin had been darker than his sister's, his hair white-blond with a cowlick that refused to flatten, even with pomade. He'd been a king at marbles and could run like the devil. He'd had a talent for the piano, too, just like their mother, but hadn't liked her Brahms and Beethoven and instead insisted on making up his own, funny little tunes with lyrics to match. A whole little life that had just – stopped.

And now, as I write *this*, this essay, I am in a new, strange place. I am slowly driving through the cemetery with my daughter Caitlin. Caitlin was born with cystic fibrosis, a genetic lung disease, and the years of infections have finally caught up with her. She's on oxygen full time, and for the past three months, she has been on the lung transplant waiting list. We are confined to Boston, knowing that the "call" could come at any time. It's summer. The city is stifling, and so we seek out bucolic adventures: the Esplanade for its river light, the Public Garden for ducklings and flowers, the Arnold Arboretum.

This trip to Mount Auburn is different. We are visiting with an oxygen tank. We cannot really pretend that we are here to seek out warblers or Song Sparrows, or to identify black gum trees. Most of the birds have left their nests now, anyway, and as beautiful as the grounds are, we can hear traffic from the nearby roads.

Yet – the peace and beauty here, the pure abundance of nature, works a calming magic. And we talk, without anxiety, about what she wants, about what I want, when the time comes. And it is this, we decide: a cemetery like Mount Auburn, a timeless place of beauty in a temporary world.

Phil Ellin

Ruby-crowned Kinglet

Fox Sparrow

American Goldfinch, male

Great Blue Heron with fish

Great Blue Heron with frog

Great Blue Heron with frog

Red-eyed Vireo

Belted Kingfisher

Sandra Lee

Heaven's Playground

The day I first set foot inside Mount Auburn Cemetery isn't one I will forget anytime soon. It was nearly two decades ago when my then-fiancé suggested the location for a Saturday afternoon rendezvous. Because I'm an individual so fearful of death, I questioned the mindset of the man whom I believed to know me so well. I was apprehensive, to say the least, about a meeting inside a cemetery.

I knew little about the place often called Sweet Auburn, in tribute to an eighteenth-century poet. Goldsmith, in "The Deserted Village," so somberly portrayed the tale of a beloved French land detached from its people, and Sweet Auburn was the fictional name given to that land. I also knew that some of the world's most intriguing individuals were buried there. Still, the idea of visiting the cemetery sent chills down my spine. In spite of my phobias however, I took a leap of faith. It was one which left my life forever changed.

A grand wrought iron gate offered a broad pavement driveway as well as a generous pedestrian entranceway. It also served as the only barrier between the bustling city streets and a whole different world – one of such sanctity I could only have imagined to exist.

Immediately captivated by the beauty which surrounded me, I forgot all about my fiancé and our plans.

First to catch my eye was a grand chapel whose exterior was constructed of marble and granite. Decorated with towering stained glass windows, the alluring structure begged visitors to step inside. Just as I was about to do so, the abundant activity throughout the cemetery drew my attention away from the multi-faceted gem. Hills of winding roads were plentiful and crowded with people on foot and in strollers. I wondered if the great energy present in the air was generated by these individuals, or by the vast forestry and wildlife which enveloped us all.

Thousands of trees consisting of hundreds of species were said by a passerby to have been imported from all over the world – trees that now house and feed a wide variety of birds, both seasonal visitors and year-round residents.

Squirrels and chipmunks wore puffed cheeks while they took from the nutrient-rich underbrush in preparation for the winter ahead. Some frolicked carelessly upon monuments and statues of all different shapes and sizes and materials. Collectively, these memorials portrayed the single idea of departure while individually they entombed thousands of stories. Each one represented a life as unique as its appearance.

Bewildered, I wandered about until I stumbled upon a wedding party. The group was posed upon a bridge before a photographer. Beneath the bridge was a pond full of lily pads which drifted in time with the movement of marine life beneath the water's surface. I looked around the grounds and realized the majority of visitors were carrying cameras and binoculars. Lovers of natural beauty enjoyed magnified views of thriving horticulture, while wildlife enthusiasts waited patiently to capture magical moments of the Downy Woodpecker or the Tufted Titmouse.

When something began tapping at my pant leg, I expected to look down at a lost child in need of assistance. Instead, I would explain to four wild turkeys that I had no food to offer them and that I was expected elsewhere. I then pulled a folded piece of paper from my back pocket. It was one upon which my fiancé had earlier scribbled directions to our meeting place. A closer look at his words suggested I would embark more upon a scavenger hunt than a leisurely stroll to find the needle in the haystack. While I enjoyed the aroma of a nearby eucalyptus, I studied what appeared to be clues.

The autocrat at the breakfast table,
wash your hands whenever you're able.

Beaten 'til the cane broke in two,
so many enemies this senator knew.

One if by land and two if by sea,
he once asked of Appleton "Marry me?"

Because the revolution had torn it down,
this man was asked to rebuild the town.

While the president was assassinated by his brother,
this actor would save the life of another.

A Venetian villa her home became,
it remains a museum bearing her name.

Many illnesses upon her did lurch,
this founder of the Christian Science Church.

Named his junior, this son of Slim,
his senate re-election did Kennedy win.

Booth, Bulfinch, Eddy, Gardner, Sumner, Lodge, Holmes, and Longfellow, I remembered, were all buried here. Because I would need guidance in locating these gravesites I retrieved a map of the grounds from the cemetery's office. After visiting each one in the order they were referenced, I wondered what next to do. I took another look at the folded piece of paper and realized I hadn't finished reading.

What I would never have had the sense to do,
my grandmother found a way.

When she first arrived here from Ireland,
she promised a note to pay.

She knew not what America for her family had in store,
so a happily ever after-life she wanted to ensure.

It took until the day I was born on her promise to make good,
and I now hold in my hand the very deed she said I would.

As you stand beneath the willow tree and stare about the grounds,
I'll ask you now to look elsewhere – to simply turn around

Across the road behind me was yet another headstone. It stood beneath an elder Oak, gracefully enveloped in swirling ivy and nestled between two Arborvitaes. Just yards away from the stone sat another of the cemetery's four bodies of water, Willow Pond. Etched upon the face of the stone was what would soon be my married name, while its backside offered more words.

I'll likely be the first to go and that's okay by me.
I know you'll join me here one day, and for eternity.

Tears filled my eyes while I studied the aged granite slab. Everything I represented, appreciated and enjoyed in life was located right here inside this sanctuary. My love for history was entertained, as was my appreciation for fine arts and literature. My desire to become more knowledgeable about matters of horticulture, agriculture and architecture would herein be met. My inherent need to be one with nature and my undying love for all walks of wildlife would be satisfied on these very grounds. The idea that I would be laid to rest here was incomprehensible.

To simply refer to this place as a cemetery by any name, I decided, was unjust. It had more to offer in life and in death than any other place on earth. It was nothing shy of what I imagined a playground in heaven to be.

Tufted Titmouse. Photo by John Harrison.

Edith Maxwell

My First Time

My hours spent ambling the paths of Mount Auburn Cemetery have been filled with many firsts. Some years ago, when I lived in Cambridge and worked in Waltham, I passed by this treasure many times every week, often on my bicycle as I rode to and from my job. I frequently stopped into the cemetery for a quiet respite from my bumpy, noisy commute.

I've been an avid birder for many decades, and used to attend daily spring warbler walks on the grounds led by experts from the Brookline Bird Club. I saw my first Great Horned Owl sitting erect in a tree across the pond. It trained its yellow eyes on our group, letting us feast our human eyes on it, then it swiveled its catlike head in regal disdain. I was hugely thrilled to have that chance to study this bird, who obligingly sat there and did not fly away so we were able to view its nearly two-foot tall form from many perspectives. To see a bird in Cambridge that one might expect to find only in remote woods was a special experience that I've never forgotten.

On another walk in the summer, I caught a flash of brilliant near-turquoise blue and then found it in my binoculars as the five-inch bird sat on a branch. I paged through my bird guide until I identified it as a male Indigo Bunting, the first sighting of another life bird for me. What a gorgeous bird it is. Its head is an iridescent darker blue that lightens into the turquoise body with darker wing stripes. I've only seen Indigo Buntings twice since then.

At that time, I was consorting with a man many years older than I. We were an unlikely pair and the relationship didn't last more than a couple of years, but he was the sweetest man I have ever been with and I was happy. We received our share of stares in public at times, because he really was old enough to be my father. But when we walked hand in hand along the paths of Mount Auburn, the birds and shrubs didn't care about the differences in our hair color, our skin textures, or our life experiences. We would search out gravestones of couples with a similar spread of ages and muse about their long-ago marriages. Other than in the privacy of home, the cemetery was the first place in which I felt truly relaxed with my beau.

I am a native Californian, and seeing a graveyard with such varied and beautiful plantings was also a first. In southern California the cemeteries tend to be grand green expanses of non-native grass maintained at a huge cost of water and chemicals. The hundreds of tree and plant species at Mount Auburn reminded me of the Los Angeles County Arboretum and Botanic Garden in Arcadia, with its vast gardens and tangled jungles of imported trees and plants, where I took nature classes as a child and learned that Hollywood movies had been filmed there.

Despite all my meanderings through Mount Auburn, I had never been to a funeral or burial there and had never ventured inside any of the buildings. The first and only time was several years ago when a cousin died too young at seventy. Like me, Mike had made the reverse migration east from California, and he also loved Mount Auburn Cemetery. His wife Catharine held his memorial service in Story Chapel, with a following reception in Bigelow Chapel up the road. Both of those beautiful buildings hosted a sad and joyous celebration of his seventy years, with relatives and friends filling the seats, sharing memories and hugs.

I'm not sure what my next Mount Auburn first will be. Come to think of it, I've never set a mystery story there. Yet.

Susan Moses

Life Among the Dead: The Magic of Mount Auburn Cemetery

Before I became a regular visitor to Mount Auburn, I never used to frequent cemeteries unless I had to. I associated cemeteries with death and dying, sadness and loss – part of the cycle of life, yes, but no need to spend extra time in them until you had to. When I attended a funeral or visited the graves of family members who had passed away, I never lingered too long. But that all changed when I discovered Mount Auburn Cemetery and its other residents – those who were very much alive. Until then I never realized how full of life a cemetery could be.

In fact, it was the chance to see raptors that brought me back to Mount Auburn. I had visited the cemetery once before, years ago when I first moved to town. I was checking out the local sights in Cambridge, the way one does when first moving into a neighborhood. I thought Mount Auburn was beautifully landscaped, and appreciated the historic significance of many of its well-known (but dead) inhabitants, but at the end of the day, it was still a burial ground to me. It wasn't until years later, when I had heard that a pair of Red-tailed Hawks had made their home there for years, that I decided to take another look.

One of my very first sightings of a newly fledged Red-tailed Hawk at Mount Auburn was also one of the strangest I've ever seen. There, in an open grassy area, was a young hawk, lying on the ground on its belly with its wings spread out, flat as a pancake. At first I thought it was hurt (or worse), but then it moved and I soon realized it was just sunning itself, resting and drying out from an early morning shower. How sweet and innocent young raptors can be – not knowing enough to be afraid of being so vulnerable. I soon came to realize, however, that it was the specialness of Mount Auburn that allowed this young hawk to grow up relatively secure and protected.

And just like that it was as if a switch had been turned on, illuminating the life within the cemetery – and I was hooked. Mount Auburn Cemetery, I discovered, was not just for the dead; it was very much alive – teeming with life in fact. From that day on Mount Auburn became a magical place for me, a place to visit my new-found feathered friends who called Mount Auburn their home. They claimed their territories, courted one another, built nests, raised young – and then did it all over again year after year. Being able to watch the dynamic of the family unit play out was an added bonus.

One warm August evening, while making our last rounds through the cemetery before closing time, a few of us came upon a rather odd scene. On the ground, just visible from the safe cover of a bush, stood a juvenile Red-tailed Hawk with its hackles up, all puffed out and mantling its wings in a defensive posture. It was calling, but it didn't sound happy. As we watched it stand there, our eyes scanned the surrounding area, and to our amazement, there stood the young hawk's father several feet away. He too was all puffed out, looking as large as I had ever seen him. Father and child were motionless, locked in a staring match. Even more surprising, however, was the dead squirrel that was sprawled on the ground between them. What had just happened? We clearly had arrived in the middle of an ongoing drama. It appeared that this was a dispute over the freshly killed squirrel, but it was unclear who had killed it and who was going to claim it. The standoff continued, mostly in silence, but every now and then the silence was pierced by an irritated cry. The mother hawk soon appeared in a nearby tree overlooking the battleground. I got the feeling that a major life lesson was being taught at this very moment, but I just wasn't sure what that lesson was – and who was teaching whom. Was the parent reprimanding the juvenile or was the juvenile showing its independence, standing its ground and not backing down? The father, still maintaining his impressive posturing stance, slowly started to approach his offspring on foot. The juvenile slowly backed up, appearing to take cover underneath a nearby bush. Vocalizations were made by both parties, but what were they saying? Eventually the father flew up to a nearby branch to join his mate, and they both seemed to continue to admonish their offspring. And all the while the poor dead squirrel, who most likely was the cause of this confrontation, remained untouched. It was a Mount Auburn moment.

Despite the graves and tombstones everywhere, it is often easy to forget that Mount Auburn is, in fact, a cemetery. But every now and then I do think about those buried beneath my feet and ponder about their lives. What was it like living in the 1800s I wonder? I read the engravings on the tombstones and marvel at those who lived a long life despite the lack of modern medicine's life-extending elixirs and procedures. But I also lament those who never got the chance to grow up, perhaps succumbing to a childhood disease that is preventable today. It reminds me of the randomness of life – and death. I want to believe that those buried here would be pleased to know that so many people come to enjoy all the living going on around them.

There is definitely something magical about Mount Auburn that screams "life" and not "death." It is alive with hawks and owls, coyotes and rabbits, chipmunks and squirrels, raccoons and groundhogs. There are Great Blue Herons and Green Herons, not to mention the catbirds and cardinals, and mockingbirds, to name just a few. And then there are the migrants who come through every spring and fall, stopping to rest and feast before continuing on their long journeys north and south.

Of course there are the beautiful trees as well – the scarlett oaks, the weeping beeches, the white pines and spruces, plus the flowering fruit trees and shrubs of all kind. Mount Auburn is literally filled with life. And you never know when you might encounter a magical moment.

As dusk approached one September evening, I spotted the resident Great Horned Owl in one of his usual trees in the Dell. He was partially hidden as was often the case when I checked on him, but I was happy to have found him. He slowly opened his bright yellow eyes and turned his head, a slow swivel around to check out his surroundings. It was getting close to his hour of departure. He soon began his wake-up routine – stretching each wing and leg together as a unit, first one side, then the other – both legs and wings probably stiff from his having slept on his perch all day. He coughed up a pellet to make room for this night's dinner and started his preening. He did a thorough cleaning, straight down to his talons, had a good shakeout, voided, and then aligned his feathers back in place. He was ready for the night. After a few deep low hoots that went unanswered, at least to my human ears, he took off, silently passing overhead and disappearing out of sight into the night. Just where does he go and what does he do all night I wondered? But that was to remain a mystery. I listened for him and tried to follow his flight, but to no avail. I walked to where I thought he had flown, but he wasn't there. Disappointed, I continued on the path where I had last seen him, and as I rounded the corner, there in front of me on the ground was a feather, a beautiful owl feather. I wanted to believe that it was a sign for me, letting me know that he had just passed by on the way to his mysterious nighttime activities that I could not be a part of.

The Cemetery has a life cycle of its own with a constantly changing cast of characters that come and go with the seasons. Winter is my favorite time of year at Mount Auburn. The crowds have thinned as have the leaves on the trees. The days are short and the air is cold and crisp. When the first snow arrives the cemetery transforms into a wintry scene right out of a Currier and

Ives print. It is a simple, stark beauty – a bright red cardinal peeking out of a snow-covered evergreen. You can hear the silence, broken periodically by the call of a blue jay scolding its arch-enemy – a Red-tailed Hawk. Bare branches reveal hidden nests, whose occupants left months ago to make their way in the world.

I love the Dell in winter. If you get there first thing in the morning after a snowfall it is beautiful – so peaceful and quiet, with the tree boughs hanging low from the load of the newly fallen snow. But the stillness belies the fact that even in the dead of winter, there is a lot of living going on. If you look closely, you might just see who has passed through. Early one morning, after an overnight snowfall, I was surprised to see so much nonhuman foot traffic. Fresh tracks revealed that the rabbits had been out, as had the coyote, and a raccoon or two had passed by as well. Looking up at the row of evergreens I noticed the snow was disturbed on a high tree branch where I assumed the owl or a hawk had perched for a bit.

Every now and then you might come across the sight of a recent life and death confrontation – where predator met prey. The tracks in the snow just stop and the snow cover is disturbed, showing signs of a struggle. A tinge of red is a sad reminder that the fight for survival in the wild is often a zero-sum game – eat or be eaten. One dies so that another may live. Death – and life – so intimately entwined.

Spring arrives at Mount Auburn as the last traces of snow and ice are melting away, uncovering the familiar paths and gravestones that had disappeared beneath the wintry covering. The chipmunks are slowly awakening from their winter hibernation and the squirrels are out in full force. The days grow longer and the earth springs to life. Bright green shoots appear out of the ground, new leaves start to unfurl on the trees, and delicate buds begin to open, giving way to the most wonderful fragrances. The air is perfumed with the likes of lilacs and lily of the valley. And with this rebirth comes the much anticipated spring migration. The warblers arrive, and with them, their admirers – busloads of them. Mount Auburn truly comes to life now, challenging everyone to keep up with all the activity.

When the migration comes to an end, and we say goodbye to our colorful visitors and bid them a good breeding season up north, the cemetery returns to a somewhat slower pace. But for some, the action is just beginning as the mating season is in full swing. While we were chasing migrating warblers, the resident birds were settling down. Territories were being claimed and defended, nests were being built or refurbished, and partners courted. If you're lucky, you might see a hawk fly by with a branch in tow – a sure sign that a nest is under construction.

As spring eases into summer, Mount Auburn is awash with new life – baby rabbits abound as do young chipmunks and squirrels. Mother birds are incubating their eggs and then feeding their open-mouthed hatchlings. And in what seems like a few short weeks, the young chicks have fledged. Most are still dependent on their parents for food so the air is filled with the sound of begging calls. The cemetery is a wonderful playground for the young hawks, who often land atop gravestones, looking as if they are living statues. And you can always count on them to surprise you.

One hot summer day I went to the top of the Dell, below the tower, for refuge from the heat and humidity. I soon discovered that I was not the only one with that idea. There, facing me, posing up close and personal, was a beautiful juvenile Red-tailed Hawk. It was sitting up tall on the railing with its leg stretched out, hanging over the bar, looking as if it were the most natural thing in the world to be resting there. I looked at the hawk and the hawk looked at me – and neither of us moved. After it finished its stretch and pulled its leg back in, it flew down the railing a bit and turned around with its back to me and stretched out its wings to catch the sun. And there it sat, spread out and relaxed, unafraid of me – an innocent's trust. It was just the two of us, alone, yet together. That, too, is the magic of Mount Auburn.

By late summer, a sultry calm descends on the cemetery. The fledglings have grown and hopefully have learned the secrets to survival. And then one day you come and can't find them. While it is sad to see them go, you wish them well, and soon begin to think about next year.

In autumn the cemetery is ablaze with color – the brilliant reds and yellows, the rich oranges and browns, punctuated with the deep greens – making every vista a painting to behold. The heat and humidity have subsided, giving way to a slight chill in the air. And the pace is different. There is a palpable sense that time is short to prepare for the approaching cold months ahead. The stragglers, those birds trying to squeeze every last minute of warm weather out of autumn, finally take off for points south, while the squirrels and blue jays are busy collecting their acorns and other food stores. The days grow shorter and the temperatures dip downward as autumn quietly slides into winter.

And so the cycle of life at Mount Auburn Cemetery continues.

Unlike my very first visit to Mount Auburn, whenever I decide to visit these days I am always thinking about what birds might be out and about, what trees and flowers are in bloom, and what nests might be occupied. Will the Great Horned Owl be sleeping in the Dell? Will I find any of the Red-tailed Hawks or get a sighting of the elusive coyote? My thoughts are almost always about life, not death. How many times have I said "I'm going to Mount Auburn," leaving off "Cemetery" as if it has no real significance? I used to wonder how it could be that on most days I simply forget that Mount Auburn is a cemetery filled with the deceased. But now I know that that is the magic of Mount Auburn. It is a sanctuary for the living – and all you have to do is just take the time to look and really see, to hear and really listen to, all the living going on.

Christopher Keane

Under the Egyptian Gate

Whenever I am impatient, especially with a book or film script, a relationship, an irksome neighbor – any frustration that leaves me torn between allowing the problem to sit by itself in peace for a time or nitpicking it to distraction – it's time for a walk.

A few weeks ago, on a Monday, I was standing at the picture window in my living room. In one hour, at the entrance to Mount Auburn Cemetery, I was to deliver a book manuscript I had edited to its author, my friend A.J.

I climbed into my warmest clothes: hat, boots, and heavy gloves. It was four degrees outside, not to mention the wind chill factor.

Should I drive, I wondered? The cemetery was only twenty-five minutes away by foot, which meant slogging through the thigh-high snow, over slick ice and through a darkness creeping in, and it was just after one. It was one of those days when I hate the weather.

The other option was a warm car and the sound track from *Lawrence of Arabia* and a drive back with the same. There's something feverish about marching across a desert in the middle of winter.

I pulled the hood over my head, plugged in my ear buds and

started out. There's nothing like a walk to Mount Auburn Cemetery, which, in my anticipation, is almost as exciting as the reality of being there. It's the difference between holding my breath and expending it, along with all the pent-up tension clogging its pathway.

I chose Mount Auburn specifically to meet A.J. But I'm getting ahead of myself.

What better a force than nature itself? Up ahead I could see through the lightly falling snow Mount Auburn's Egyptian gate, the curtain between streams of rumbling, coughing traffic and the serene, perpetual presence of nature.

The official start of every walk takes place under the Egyptian gate where, by habit – one of many that have originated at Mount Auburn and carried out wherever I've traveled – I stop and silently mouth one of the most environmental, and shortest, of poems. It's by Ogden Nash:

> I think that I shall never see
> a billboard lovely as a tree.
> Perhaps, unless the billboards fall,
> I'll never see a tree at all.

My first task this Monday was to deliver the package under my arm to my friend, A.J., an Egyptian-born M.D. who taught at Harvard and has a practice in Boston. A.J. was the most passionate practitioner of his medical craft that I have ever known.

A.J. told me the Friday before that his anxiety soared higher than the moon when he received a call that morning from one of the titans of the book business. A.J.'s brother was a personal friend of this titan and asked him to read his brother's novel. The titan said he would get to it immediately.

When I saw A.J. that Friday I congratulated him and told him to send off the manuscript. But he hesitated and said, "I'm not at all sure it's right." "Right?" I asked him. "About what?" "I know you have spent many hours with this already, Chris, but could you please, please, read it one more time?"

Even though I'd read six previous versions over the past three years, I said I would. A.J. said, "Oh, I am so grateful." He whipped out the manuscript and handed it to me with a smile. "In case you said yes I brought it with me. I'll need it by Monday. I'll get it from you then and send it right off. The fellow wanted it right away." He said he'd meet me wherever I'd like.

Monday, I thought, sure, why not. I'd have to cancel, postpone, or reschedule meetings, a dinner party, and a school play. But this was really important to A.J. He had toiled like a Dickensian scrivener over three years and this was, as we both knew, a once-in-a-lifetime opportunity.

But wait, I thought, what about any changes? How would he…? But A.J. was already on his way, literally dancing away. I left a message on his phone to meet back under the Egyptian arch on Monday. Just in case.

While he left for Mount Auburn Hospital, I decided to find a place on the cemetery grounds to start his novel. The snowfall was more like a dusting, so it shouldn't have been difficult.

Soon I came upon the gravestone of Henrietta Goddard Wigglesworth, wife of Alexander Porter, but it was not the gravestone that I wanted to lean against to read his book. It was what lay behind the gravestone: a bassinette made of the same stone – a covered bassinette, elegant, tufted, but not large enough for me to rest in. I thought, "If only it were a little bigger." But I wouldn't have chanced it anyway. Why tempt the other inhabitants?

I stood there for a while. Above, the gray color of the sky matched that of the gravestone. I opened A.J.'s novel. He had told me about some of the changes since I read it last. I was back with the young Egyptian girl living with her father, a poor farmer, and her pet bull. Right away he had me interested; A.J. had brought me to a small village in India and there I remained for ninety pages.

Time has a way of vanishing in Mount Auburn. It's no more than a concept that we refer to beyond the cemetery's borders. But if I'm walking through Mount Auburn and have an appointment, I find myself almost automatically closing up whatever I'm doing and leaving the cemetery to somehow arrive at the appointment exactly when I'm supposed to.

I spent the next seventy pages strolling, stopping, and picking up the pace, all with regard to what I was reading. For instance, when the young girl's bull breaks free from her home and tears through the streets, I found myself almost galloping along one of the multitude of paths.

How often have we heard that expression about losing your patience? At Mount Auburn I don't lose it. As soon as I enter the cemetery I gain it back. I'll lose it out there among the four-wheeled mechanisms dashing about, but the moment I cross under the arch, a peace washes over me. There are some expressions that seem to have been forbidden at Mount Auburn: "Hurry up!" "There's no time!" "Let's go! We're late!"

On Sunday morning I returned to Mount Auburn and under the Washington Tower I finished A.J.'s book. Beautifully written from the soul of the young Egyptian girl who loses her father, a young French soldier, and her bull. One of the saddest stories I'd ever read. It was haunting, and passionate, and it needed work.

So here we are back beneath the Egyptian gate. It is Monday and here comes A.J. who says, "If you hate it, don't tell me." "No," I replied, "in fact, I liked it." "Did you read it here?" he asked. "Most of it," I said. A.J. looked around. "You read it here? How? It's so quiet." A.J. laughed.

"So," A.J. said. "I'll send it off. The post office is just down…" "Not yet," I said. A.J.'s eyes widened, as eyes do when they suspect that life is about to take a sudden turn for the worse. "It's a good book," I said to him, and added, "but you still have three or four large holes to plug, plus the spelling mistakes, and the grammar also needs to be cleaned up. It shouldn't take…" "How long?" he said, starting to shake. "The way you work, A.J.," I said, "no more than a couple of months."

A.J.'s upper lip quivered. His tongue ran across his teeth. He raised his soupy eyes to the landscape as if it were the first time he actually looked at the majestic nature as it rose up around him.

"I have a confession to make," he said. "Oh?" "Oh, Chris," he said, "on Friday after I handed you my novel… I found myself passing the post office. I don't know what happened, but I took an extra copy of the manuscript I had into the post office and… sent it to the publisher. Overnight."

After a long pause, I said, "You didn't." "I'm afraid so. All weekend I have been punishing myself."

I thought, But did you have to punish me? I had to change last minute plans at least a half-dozen times. I worked very hard, for what? For a moment I was shocked, then angry, and quickly my "I…I…me" focus vanished and went where it belonged, on A.J.

The only hope A.J. had was that the publishing titan overlooked what I saw, or perhaps I was mistaken and he accepted it. I did know that I must have felt something amiss when I asked A.J. to meet me under the Egyptian arch, where problems never seem so problematic any more.

I asked A.J. to take a walk with me through the cemetery. He said he was late for a very important appointment, and rushed off.

The publishing titan passed on A.J.'s book, without going into detail about why, other than it wasn't right for him.

A.J. has continued to rewrite, and I continue to spend early afternoons under Mount Auburn's Egyptian gate.

Mary Pinard

Direct Address

All who enter you, Sweet Auburn – new widow, grieving parent,
bereft friend, or otherwise engaged birder, ears tuned, eyes keen
    to trees, whether
curtained with leaves in spring, or bare in fall, thanks to autumn
    winds – all take
delight in your all, the fact of your urban address only
enhancing your nature, art: the Egyptian Revival Gatehouse, a
    quiet
finesse in its austere and faithful columns of
granite, most perfect stone, bone of deepest earth
hewn for your entryway – dignified, and humble too – or your
iconic American *Sphinx*, Milmore's triumph, where else such a
    force for
justice, memorial to slavery abolished, body of a lion, face of a
    woman, a
kilter of perfect dimensions, or your chapels, Bigelow and Story,
    your overlooks and
lakes, your monuments to the famed – Eddy, Shaw, Franklin,
    Gray – or your
making famous the ordinary, or forgotten – martyr, unknown
    soldier, pet – and your
naming in carved emblems the lives of the dead: weaver, father,
    virgin, infant, senator,
ornithologist, poet, and what of your welcome to birds and birds
    and birds, the steadfast

permanent residents – Gulls and Starlings, Waxwings and the
quintessential Hawks, Mockingbirds and
Robins, Titmice and Owls – and the ever-many
species of migrating warblers, always it seems on the wing,
    Blackpoll,
Tennessee, Blackburnian, Yellow, Magnolia, Palm, though that
    leaves
unnoted the much rarer Cerulean, Hooded, and Mourning, and
    those who
visit just long enough to rear their young – Belted Kingfisher,
    Song Sparrow,
Warbling Vireo, oh Sweet Auburn, your avenues and paths map
    our own
Xanadu. Tome of lone passages,
you are an alphabet that reinvents us with a
zillion new ways to say life.

Red-tailed Hawk with prey. Photo by Kim Nagy.

Spring Migrants and Other Favorites

By John Harrison

Hooded Warbler

Golden-crowned Kinglet

Rose-breasted Grosbeak

Ruby-crowned Kinglet

Scarlet Tanager

Yellow-bellied Sapsucker

Common Yellowthroat

Nashville Warbler

Black-billed Cuckoo

Black-throated Blue Warbler

Blue-winged Warbler

Brown Thrasher

Cerulean Warbler

Hermit Thrush

Ruby-throated Hummingbird

Magnolia Warbler

Red-bellied Woodpecker

Red-eyed Vireo

Cedar Waxwing

Red-winged Blackbird

Contributor Biographies

Peter Alden

Peter Alden, of Concord, MA, is a past president of both the Nuttall Ornithological Club and the Brookline Bird Club. He has led bird and nature tours, cruises, safaris, and private jet trips to over one hundred countries and the seven seas. His fifteen published books on birds and travel have sold over two million copies, including his *National Audubon Field Guide to New England*. He is currently a study leader for Road Scholar's A-Team on small- and medium-sized cruises to Africa, Alaska, the Amazon, Central America, Antarctica, and the Antilles.

David Barnett

Dave has been at Mount Auburn Cemetery for 22 years, having started in 1993 as Director of Horticulture. He was promoted to Vice President of Operations and Horticulture in 1999, and became President and CEO in 2008. Prior to Mount Auburn, Dave was Assistant Director at Planting Fields Arboretum in Oyster Bay, New York, from 1986 to 1993. He has held various other positions in the field of public horticulture.

Dave's educational background includes a BS in environmental horticulture from the University of Connecticut, and an MS in environmental horticulture and a PhD in ecology from the University of California, Davis.

Dave served for 9 years on the Board of Directors of the American Public Gardens Association (APGA), including a two-year term as President. In 2013 he received APGA's Honorary Life Member Award, the Association's most prestigious award.

He served 2 years as President of the Horticultural Club of Boston.

Upton Bell

Upton Bell has been a radio and television personality in New England for the past thirty-eight years, beginning in 1977 at WBZ with *Calling All Sports* with Bob Lobel. Bell has hosted such shows as Channel 38's *Sports Beat*, WEEI's *Sports Line*, and the first national NFL draft show in 1977 on PBS. In 1990, he transitioned from sports talk to general talk, succeeding Dave Maynard on WBZ radio. Bell's WTAG show was recognized by the Associated Press for Outstanding Talk Show in New England for three consecutive years. Bell has interviewed President George W. H. Bush (at the White House), President Bill Clinton, Secretary of State Henry Kissinger, Secretary of State John Kerry, Senator Ted Kennedy, Speaker of the House Tip O'Neill, Ambassador to the Vatican Ray Flynn, scientist Stephen Hawking, Harvard Law Professor Alan Dershowitz, and award-winning authors such as Doris Kearns Goodwin, David McCullough, Stephen King, Norman Mailer, and William Martin.

Bell's career started in 1961 with the Baltimore Colts of the National

Football League. He rose to become the director of player personnel. During his tenure, the Colts went to two NFL conference championships and two Super Bowls, winning the 1970 Super Bowl over the Dallas Cowboys. Bell became the youngest general manager in pro football when he was named general manager of the New England Patriots in 1971 at the age of thirty-three. He is the son of Bert Bell, founder of the Philadelphia Eagles and commissioner of the NFL from 1946 to 1959. His mother, Frances Upton, was a Broadway actress and Ziegfeld Follies star.

Connie Biewald

Connie Biewald teaches and writes in Cambridge, MA. She is the author of three novels – *Digging to Indochina*, *Bread and Salt*, and *Roses Take Practice* – and is at work on a fourth, *Heart of the Yam*.

Je Anne Strott-Branca

Je Anne Strott-Branca has served the Red Rock Audubon Society in Las Vegas, NV, in many capacities. She has been interim president (May and June 2014), vice president (two different terms), treasurer, and education chairperson. She has also served many years as field trip chair and is currently the Whittel Fund chair. Two of her articles about birding the Henderson Bird Viewing Preserve have been published in *Birder's World* magazine (August 2007), and an article about birding Tule Springs in Las Vegas was published in *BirdWatching* magazine (June 2013 – same magazine but new name). She was also featured in an article about birding in Delta Airline's *Sky* magazine (December 2005). Je Anne was instrumental in the development and printing of the Birding Trail Map from Henderson to Laughlin, NV. She worked for eleven years (after retiring in 2002) at the Henderson Bird Viewing Preserve and developed and taught Beginning Birding and Birding 101 classes in addition to some others. Je Anne was a docent at the Memphis Zoo and Aquarium in Memphis, TN, for fifteen years. She has traveled to all fifty states, Mexico, Canada, Puerto Rico, Costa Rica, Panama, South Africa, Australia, New Zealand, Fiji, American Samoa, and New Caledonia.

Ray Brown

Ray Brown is the creator and host of the *Talkin' Birds* radio show, heard on fourteen stations in New England, New York, and Maryland, and internationally via iTunes and *Talkinbirds.com*. He's also a music host for Classical 99.5 WCRB in Boston (part of the WGBH family) and the narrator for Simon & Schuster's Pimsleur Language Programs. Ray has been a top-five national finalist in "Air Personality of the Year" competitions from *Billboard* and the National Association of Broadcasters; his "Back Seat Governor" radio promotion was featured in a *Time* photo story; he has received a National Association of Auto Dealers "Chassie" Award for radio commercial performance; and his novelty record "Get Preppy (The Preppy Song)" was played on radio stations in major markets including Boston, Cleveland, St. Louis, and Detroit.

Pierce Butler

Pierce Butler is the author of the novel, *A Riddle of Stars*, and numerous stories and essays. He teaches writing and literature at Bentley University, and is working on an historical novel set in Ireland and North America during the Irish Potato Famine of the 1840s. He has traveled extensively in Mount Auburn Cemetery.

Shawn Carey

Shawn Carey (Migration Productions) produces bird/wildlife-related multi-media presentations, videos, and photo workshops that have been presented at many natural history events all over the United States. Shawn moved from his home in Erie, PA, in October 1986 to Cambridge, MA, and started watching birds in 1988. In 1991, Shawn began to combine his interest in photography with his interest in birds. By 1994, he and good friend Jim Grady started Migration Productions as a way to show their multi-image slide presentations to live audiences. Since then, Migration Productions has been presenting programs to natural history and birding organizations and camera clubs. He is the past president and current vice president of the Eastern Massachusetts Hawk Watch, and is on the Advisory Council for Mass Audubon. Shawn's photos have been published in *The Boston Globe*, *The New York Times*, *Sanctuary* (the magazine of the Massachusetts Audubon Society), *Science*, *Hawk Mountain News* (the magazine of the Hawk Mountain Sanctuary), and many others over the past eighteen-plus years. In 1997 he started teaching bird photography workshops (Fundamentals of Bird Photography) for the Massachusetts Audubon Society.

Douglas E. Chickering

Doug Chickering has spent almost half his life birding, having first been exposed to it in 1979. His working life consists of being an architectural model maker, an industrial model maker, an engineering piping model maker, and a master machinist for a medical device company (which is a progression, of sorts). As a child he spent his summers on the Parker River in Newbury, MA, and has lived either there or in nearby Groveland, MA, since 1982.

Robert "Boz" Cogan

Robert "Boz" Cogan has been an avid photographer since 2003. For medical reasons, he was advised to walk for his health. On his daily walks for exercise, he started to notice his surroundings and decided he wanted to share what he'd seen. His favorite places to photograph in Massachusetts are Mount Auburn Cemetery in Cambridge; Horn Pond in Woburn; Salisbury Beach, Plum Island, Cape Ann, and Jeffries Point in East Boston (for the Boston skyline and harbor at sunrise). In Florida, his favorite places to photograph are Sanibel Island and the southwest Florida area. His favorite subjects are flowers, wildlife, landscapes, seascapes, and anyplace or anything where water is involved.

Ray Daniel

Ray Daniel is the award-winning author of Boston-based crime fiction. His short story "Give Me a Dollar" won a 2014 Derringer Award for short fiction, and "Driving Miss Rachel" was chosen as a 2013 distinguished short story by Otto Penzler, editor of *The Best American Mystery Stories 2013*. Daniel's work has been published in the Level Best Books anthologies, *Thin Ice*, *Blood Moon*, and *Stone Cold*. *Terminated* is his first novel.

www.raydanielmystery.com
@raydanielmystery

Linda Darman

Linda Darman started out in publishing at Random House during its heyday, working for such notable editors as Toni Morrison, Nan Talese, and Jason Epstein. She then went on to a long career in non-profit administration. Darman holds a master's degree in cross-cultural studies from Boston University and has been a human rights activist with Amnesty International since 1999. She is a writer, editor, oral historian, and certified yoga instructor living in New York City and Boston's South End.

Alan M. Dershowitz

Alan M. Dershowitz, the Felix Frankfurter Professor of Law, Emeritus at Harvard Law School, is a practicing criminal and constitutional lawyer. He has been called one of the nation's most distinguished defenders of individual rights. A native of Brooklyn, NY, Professor Dershowitz is a graduate of Brooklyn College and Yale Law School. He joined the Harvard Law School faculty at age twenty-five after clerking for Judge David Bazelon and Justice Arthur Goldberg. In 1983, the Anti-Defamation League of B'nai B'rith presented Professor Dershowitz with the William O. Douglas First Amendment Award for his "compassionate eloquent leadership and persistent advocacy in the struggle for civil and human rights."

Professor Dershowitz has published more than one thousand articles in magazines, newspapers, journals, and blogs, including in *The New York Times Magazine*, *The Washington Post*, *The Wall Street Journal*, *The Harvard Law Review*, *The Yale Law Journal*, *The Huffington Post*, *Newsmax*, *The Jerusalem Post*, and *Ha'aretz*. He is the author of thirty fiction and nonfiction works with a worldwide audience, including the New York Times Number One Best Seller, *Chutzpah*, and five other national bestsellers. His autobiography, *Taking the Stand: My Life in the Law*, was published in 2013 by Crown, a division of Random House. More than a million of his books – translated into many languages – have been sold worldwide. In addition to his numerous law review articles and books about criminal and constitutional law, he has written, taught and lectured about history, philosophy, psychology, literature, mathematics, theology, music, sports – and even delicatessens. He is married to Carolyn Cohen, a PhD psychologist.

Wendy Drexler

Wendy Drexler's book-length collection, *Western Motel*, was published in April 2012 by Turning Point. Her poems have appeared in *Barrow Street, Blood Orange Review, Cider Press Review, Meatpaper, Mid-American Review, Nimrod, Peregrine, Poetry East, Tar River Poetry, Off the Coast, umbrellajournal.com*, and other journals. Her work has also been featured on *Verse Daily* and in the anthologies, *Blood to Remember: American Poets on the Holocaust* and *Burning Bright: Passager Celebrates 21 Years*. She was nominated for a Pushcart Prize in 2012 by *The Mid-American Review*, in 2011 by *Cider Press Review*, and in 2007 for her chapbook, *Drive-Ins, Gas Stations, the Bright Motels* (Pudding House). She is a poetry editor for *Sanctuary*, the magazine of the Massachusetts Audubon Society. Wendy has enjoyed walking in Mount Auburn Cemetery for years. In the mid-1990s, she watched transfixed as a Great Blue Heron patiently, and ultimately unsuccessfully, tried to swallow a frog at Willow Pond, a memory that has stayed with her ever since.
www.WendyDrexlerPoetry.com

George Ellenbogen

George Ellenbogen's poetry appears in five collections, in French and German translations, and in numerous anthologies and magazines. Véhicule Press has just released a memoir of the Montreal of his childhood and adolescence, *A Stone in My Shoe: In Search of Neighborhood*. He has read his work on both sides of the Atlantic, and is the subject of a documentary film, *George Ellenbogen: Canadian Poet in America*. Retired as a professor emeritus of creative writing, he currently lives in Boston, MA.

Phil Ellin

Phil Ellin has been involved with nature photography for over twenty-five years. He has been the recipient of many photographic awards, and his work has been published in various textbooks and magazines. Phil has also taught adult education courses and workshops in nature photography for several years. Many of his photographs are hanging in private homes and offices throughout the country.

Nancy Esposito

Nancy Esposito's most recent book is *Lamentation with June Bug* (Word Press, 2013). Her first book of poems was *Changing Hands* (Quarterly Review of Literature Contemporary Poetry Series). *Mêm' Rain*, a winner of the National Looking Glass Poetry Chapbook Competition, was published in 2002 by Pudding House Publications, which also published *Greatest Hits 1978-2001* in 2003. She received the Discovery/*The Nation* Award, Massachusetts Arts Lottery Grant, the Colladay Award, and Poetry Society of America Award. In addition, she traveled to Egypt on a Fulbright Grant; was awarded grants to visit Vietnam, Cambodia, Thailand, and Laos; and was given a grant by the National Endowment for the Humanities to study the Vietnam War. She lived in Mexico and Nicaragua in the 1980s where she translated contemporary Nicaraguan poets. Her own work has been translated into Spanish and Vietnamese.

Peter Filichia

Peter Filichia has spent most of the last forty-five years writing about theater as a critic for a daily newspaper (*The Star-Ledger* in Newark, NJ), a magazine (*TheaterWeek*), and the internet (*Playbill, Theatremania, Music Theatre International, Masterworks Broadway,* and *Kritzerland*). He is the author of *Let's Put on a Musical; The Biggest Hit of the Season/The Biggest Flop of the Season; Broadway Musicals' Most Valuable Players; Strippers, Showgirls, and Sharks;* and *The Great Parade: The Remarkable 1963-64 Broadway Season,* published in 2015. His play *Games,* about bullying, has seen high school productions in all fifty states and six foreign countries. His play *Adam's Gifts: A New Christmas Carol* was a finalist for a Terrence McNally Award. He has been president of the Drama Desk Awards and holds that post now with the Theatre World Awards. He has served as an assessor for the National Endowment for the Arts, and for the past twenty years has been the musical theater judge for the ASCAP Awards program and critic-in-residence for the University of Cincinnati – Conservatory of Music.

Kate Flora

Award-winning mystery and true crime writer Kate Flora is the author of fourteen books, including the true crime story, *Death Dealer,* and the novel, *And Grant You Peace,* both published in 2014. Her book *Finding Amy* (true crime), co-written with a Portland, ME, deputy police chief, was a 2007 Edgar Award nominee. Kate's other titles include the Thea Kozak mysteries and the starred-review Joe Burgess police series, the third of which, *Redemption,* won the 2013 Maine Literary Award for Crime Fiction. A former Maine assistant attorney general in the areas of battered children and employment discrimination, Kate is a founding member of the New England Crime Bake and Maine Crime Wave conferences, and a founder of Level Best Books where she worked as an editor and publisher for seven years. She has served as international president of Sisters in Crime. When she's not riding an ATV through the Canadian woods or hiding in a tick-infested field waiting to be found by search and rescue dogs as research for her books, she can be found teaching writing at Grub Street in Boston, MA.

Ray Flynn

Ray Flynn is the former Mayor of Boston, U.S. Ambassador to the Vatican, and author of the best-selling novel, *The Accidental Pope,* and a biography, *John Paul II: A Personal Portrait of the Pope and the Man.* He is also a leading advocate for the handicapped and special-needs children.

Before entering politics, he was an All-American basketball player at Providence College and was voted to the All American-Academic Team. In 1963 he was voted Most Valuable Player in the National Invitational

Tournament in Madison Square Garden, while leading Providence College to the national championship.

Camilla H. Fox

Camilla H. Fox is the founding executive director of Project Coyote – a national coalition of scientists and educators promoting compassionate conservation and coexistence between people and wildlife through education, science, and advocacy. She has a master's degree in wildlife ecology, policy, and conservation, and twenty years of experience working on behalf of wildlife and wildlands. Camilla's work has been featured in several films, and in *The New York Times,* the BBC, NPR, *Orion, and USA Today* magazine. A frequent speaker and blogger on these issues, Camilla has authored more than seventy publications, and is co-author of *Coyotes in Our Midst: Coexisting with an Adaptable and Resilient Carnivore*; co-editor and lead author of the book, *Cull of the Wild: A Contemporary Analysis of Trapping in the United States*; and producer of the award-winning documentary, *Cull of the Wild: The Truth Behind Trapping*. Camilla has served as an appointed member on the U.S. Secretary of Agriculture's National Wildlife Services Advisory Committee, and currently serves on several non-profit advisory boards, including Living with Wolves, the Human Wildlife Conflict Collaboration, and the Felidae Conservation Fund.

www.projectcoyote.org

John Hadidian

John Hadidian is the senior scientist for wildlife at the Humane Society of the United States (HSUS). Prior to coming to the HSUS he was a wildlife biologist with the National Park Service's Center for Urban Ecology where he conducted field research on raccoon, deer, and squirrels in urban parks. He has served on the U.S. Department of State's Man and the Biosphere Program, as a member of the Human Dominated Systems Directorate, as associate editor for the journal *Urban Ecosystems*, and as chair of the Wildlife Society's Urban Wildlife Working Group. He is the principal author of the book, *Wild Neighbors: the Humane Approach to Living with Wildlife*.

Helen Hannon

Helen Hannon holds a master's degree in writing composition and an undergraduate degree in sociology/anthropology from the University of Massachusetts, Boston. Her historical interests focus on the nineteenth century and Massachusetts during the Civil War. Her articles have appeared in national and local publications, such as the *Harvard Gazette, Ireland of the Welcomes, New England Ancestors*, and *The Journal of African-American History*. Additionally, she served on the board of the Victorian Society in America/New England Chapter, and founded a Civil War discussion group at the Boston Athenaeum Library. She spearheaded the successful preservation of the Soldiers Field Monument at Harvard University, and the Charles Russell Lowell, Post Number Seven, Grand Army of the Republic Monument located in Boston.

John Harrison

John Harrison graduated from Bentley University and then served in the U.S. Navy with the Naval Security Group. He was stationed at NAVCOMMSTA Sidi Yahia, Morocco. Returning to civilian life, he founded Epilog Enterprises, a book distribution company, in 1975. He is currently the president and works with his founding partners, Arthur and Corinne Kinsman.

It was a passing remark from one of this book's contributors, author and Bentley University professor Pierce Butler, that brought Harrison to Mount Auburn Cemetery in 2000. He had always been interested in photography, but it was Mount Auburn's wildlife that redirected his focus. It was his passion for nature that ultimately led to the idea for this book. His photographs have been published by Mass Audubon, the Humane Society of the United States, and Project Coyote in CA, and have appeared in books, magazines, newspapers, and websites. He lectures on nature and wildlife at elementary schools and to senior citizen groups. Additionally, he initiated and authored the *Medford Wildlife Watch* blog for *The Medford Transcript* newspaper for several years.

Gary Goshgarian (Gary Braver)

Gary Braver is the award-winning and bestselling author of eight critically acclaimed thrillers. His novels have been celebrated for their high concepts, careful craftsmanship, well-rounded characters, and page-turning momentum. His novel *Flashback* is the only thriller to have won the prestigious Massachusetts Book Award for Fiction. His latest novel is *Tunnel Vision*, which legendary author Ray Bradbury called "a wonderfully frightening and insightful tale." Braver's novels have been translated into seven languages, and three were optioned for movies, including *Elixir* by director Ridley Scott. He is the only thriller novelist to have three separate titles simultaneously listed in the top-ten highest customer reviews on Amazon.com. His fiction and nonfiction pieces have appeared in *The Boston Globe, The New York Times, Writer Magazine, The Christian Science Monitor*, and the Edgar-award-winning *Thriller 2 Anthology*.

Under his own name, Gary Goshgarian, he is an award-winning professor of English at Northeastern University where he teaches courses in modern bestsellers, science fiction, horror fiction, and fiction writing. He has also taught fiction-writing workshops throughout the United States as well as in England and Europe for over twenty-five years. In addition to his novels, he is the author of five popular college writing textbooks. He lives with his family outside of Boston, MA.

www.garybraver.com

Nathan Goshgarian

Nathan Goshgarian is a Massachusetts-based nature photographer. His passion for photography began while completing a master's degree in conservation biology in Australia and New Zealand. His most memorable location to photograph is Milford Sound in Fiordland, New Zealand, and his favorite subject is owls, anywhere he can find them.

Christopher Keane

Christopher Keane has practiced his impatience and on occasion overcome it to have fifteen books published, three movies made, along with a TV series and assorted speaking engagements. His first publication was as a graduate student in Blake studies under the title: "The Tyger and the Hairy Ape: What William Blake Prophesied in 'The Tyger' Eugene O'Neill Realized in *The Hairy Ape*." Chris wrote the piece in another paradise: the National Arboretum near Washington, D.C.

Gayle Lakin

Gayle Lakin is a lifelong learner who has focused on the arts and education. She is an art teacher to many young public school students and recently won an Outstanding Veteran Arts Educator Award for her school district. While her goal is to open her students' eyes to the creative process, she delights in how they are continually opening her eyes. She received a BA from the University of Rochester, spent many years at the Harvard University Ceramics Studio, earned an MFA from Cranbrook Academy of Art, an MSEd from Long Island University, and an "imaginary degree" from Mount Auburn Cemetery where she has regularly gone to collect her thoughts as soon as she was old enough to take public transportation by herself.

Sandra Lee

Sandra Lee is a Boston-based mystery and true crime writer as well as an investigative reporter often recognized by the media. Prior to beginning her writing career, Lee worked for twenty years as a legal assistant and paralegal. She is a graduate of Northeastern University, where she studied criminal justice and American history, and also obtained her paralegal certificate. Since 2009, she has penned seven novels, including her two latest, *Dirty Water* and *The Shanty: Provincetown's Lady in the Dunes*. Lee currently has two true crime works in progress: *The Writer: Revisiting the Murder of Christa Worthington* and *Deliver Us From Evil: The Horrifying True Story of Puppy Doe*. Lee visits libraries, bookstores, and community centers all over New England to speak about her books. She also volunteers her time teaching underprivileged children the art of writing.
www.sandraleebooks.com

Clare Walker Leslie

Clare Walker Leslie is a nationally known naturalist, artist, and educator. She is the author of ten books on drawing and observing nature, and teaches nature journaling across the country and to all ages. As one of the founders of Mass Audibon's Habitat Education Center and Wildlife Sanctuary, Clare began teaching nature drawing in Belmont, MA, back in 1971. Now working on her twelfth book, *Exploring Nature Where You Are*, a basic book on nature for adults, Clare is using many of her own experiences in her books as she explores the curious world just outside the door with her granddaughter. Clare lives in both Cambridge, MA, and Granville, VT, with her family and various animals.

Clare was trained in the field of drawing and painting outdoors by a number of prominent and extremely helpful teachers/colleagues and fellow adventurers: Eric Ennion (England), John Busby (Scotland), Lars Jonsson and Gunnar Brusewitz (Sweden), Don Stokes (USA), and Chris Leahy (Mass Audubon/ MA). She currently spends many hours exploring the wilds of Massachusetts and the rest of the country. An exhibition of her work appeared at the Museum of Bird Art at Mass Audubon / Canton: "Looking Closely: The Art of Observation" (September 28, 2014 to January 11, 2015). *www.clarewalkerleslie.com*

Elsa Lichman

Elsa Lichman is a retired social worker who is now a columnist for the *Waltham News Tribune*. Her regular contributions include "Nature in the City," as well as memoir, historical, and "Meet Your Neighbor" pieces. In addition, she is a poet, multi-media visual artist, singer, and musician (who plays piano, steel drum, and percussion), and she has participated in choral and theatrical productions. She has traveled extensively, including swimming with the wild humpback whales in the Silver Bank in the Caribbean and studying African dance in Senegal. After discovering Mount Auburn Cemetery forty-five years ago, she remains captivated by its wildlife, beauty, spirituality, and healing essence.

Megan Marshall

Megan Marshall, an associate professor at Emerson College, is the author of *Margaret Fuller: A New American Life*, which won the Pulitzer Prize for Biography in 2014, and *The Peabody Sisters: Three Women Who Ignited American Romanticism*, winner of the Francis Parkman Prize and the Mark Lynton History Prize and a finalist for the Pulitzer Prize in 2006. Both books received the Massachusetts Book Award in Nonfiction.

William Martin

William Martin is *The New York Times* best-selling author of ten novels, an award-winning PBS documentary, book reviews, magazine articles, and a cult-classic horror movie too. His first Peter Fallon novel, *Back Bay*, appeared in 1980. Since then, in novels like *Cape Cod*, *Citizen Washington*, and *The Lincoln Letter*, he has told the American story through the eyes of the great and the anonymous, sweeping his readers from the deck of the *Mayflower* to Civil War Washington to 9/11. *Publisher's Weekly* has called him "a storyteller whose smoothness matches his ambition." He was the 2005 recipient of the prestigious New England Book Award, given to an author "whose body of work stands as a significant contribution to the culture of the region." He lives near Boston, MA, with his wife, and has three grown children. He is currently working on his eleventh novel, *The Mother Lode*, set during the Gold Rush.

Joe Martinez

Joe Martinez has been fascinated by reptiles and amphibians since his undergraduate college days in the mid-1970s. He has worked with live reptiles and amphibians at the Franklin Park, Bronx, and Central Park Zoos. He has held a part-time staff position in the Herpetology Department of the Museum of Comparative Zoology at Harvard University since 1990 and recently ended a twelve-year stint as an outreach educator for the New England Wildlife Center in Weymouth, MA. He has a BA, an MA in teaching, and an EdD, all from Boston University.

Edith Maxwell

Former organic farmer Edith Maxwell writes the Local Foods Mysteries about farmer Cam Flaherty, a locavore club, and locally sourced murder (Kensington Publishing). She also writes the Speaking of Mystery series (Barking Rain Press, written as Tace Baker), which features Quaker linguistics professor Lauren Rousseau. Edith holds a PhD in linguistics and is a long-time Quaker. She also writes award-winning short crime fiction. A technical writer and fourth-generation Californian, she lives north of Boston, MA.

www.edithmaxwell.com   *www.facebook.com/EdithMaxwellAuthor*
www.wickedcozyauthors.com   *@edithmaxwell*

Anneliese Merrigan

Anneliese Merrigan was born in Boston, MA, and currently lives in Medford, MA. She had an interest in writing at an early age. In fourth grade her teacher recognized her curiosity and talent and carefully nurtured her progress. Her poems and stories were full of highly descriptive language and imaginative characters. It was also in fourth grade, while at Columbus Elementary School in Medford, that Anneliese was introduced to Mount Auburn Cemetery during a classroom visit from John Harrison. Later, while attending Shady Hill School in Cambridge, MA, she visited Mount Auburn regularly for science projects, art classes, and writing assignments. She remains amazed and intrigued by the flora, fauna, and gravestones of this special and venerable place. After graduating from Shady Hill School in 2014, Anneliese entered the International Baccalaureate Diploma Program at the Newman School in Boston. She enjoys writing, drawing, and photography, and is an avid guitar player, singer, and music enthusiast.

Jeffrey Scott Meshach

Jeffrey Scott Meshach was hatched and raised in Stanhope, NJ, on the banks of Lake Musconetcong. It was on and along this lake where he developed his appreciation for wildlife, with plenty of help from his father and maternal grandfather. He received his associate of arts degree from Garrett Community College in western Maryland in 1982, and his bachelor of science degree from West Virginia University in 1985. A college buddy got him interested in raptors, and he heard about what was then the Raptor Rehabilitation and Propagation Project in Missouri (now World Bird Sanctuary). From his humble beginnings as a non-paid intern, he gained knowledge in rehabilitating injured birds of prey, training and presenting live birds in education programs, participating in wild bird studies, banding birds, and many other facets of the World Bird Sanctuary.

His greatest joys in life are his children and wife, fishing and hunting, banding wild Peregrine Falcon chicks, and knowing that his life's work helps save the world's birds.

Dee Morris

Dee Morris is an independent scholar and educational consultant specializing in the nineteenth-century history of Greater Boston. She has presented many walking tours at Mount Auburn Cemetery as well as at Forest Hills Cemetery in Jamaica Plain, MA. Her programs for libraries, schools, and historical societies give people the opportunity to connect with their civic ancestors. Dee's published work includes brief histories of Medford, MA, and Somerville, MA, as well as an exploration of the golden age of spiritualism – belief in real communication with those who have passed away – in Boston and surrounding communities.

Susan Moses

Susan Moses is deputy director of the Center for Health Communication at the Harvard School of Public Health. The Center, best known for its Designated Driver Campaign, develops and implements national campaigns using traditional and social media to promote healthy behaviors and lifestyles. Prior to coming to Harvard, she worked in Washington, D.C., as an environmental policy analyst and promoted the public understanding of science. She received her undergraduate degree in chemistry from Cornell University, where she also studied animal behavior and conducted field research on Howler Monkeys in Costa Rica. She received her master's degree in health policy and management from the Harvard School of Public Health. She lives in Cambridge, MA, and is a regular visitor to Mount Auburn.

Kim Nagy

Kim Nagy has made the natural world both her profession and her hobby. She is an avid wildlife and nature photographer, and travels widely in pursuit of her craft. She works as a regional sales manager in the natural foods industry, and travels extensively throughout the East Coast and the Midwest. She graduated from Boston College, and holds the Zertifikat Deutsch als Fremdsprache from the Goethe Institut in Munich, Germany. Her photos have appeared in *National Geographic*'s Daily Dozen, *BirdWatching*, several publications of the Massachusetts Audubon Society, *The Marco Review*, and others.
www.facebook.com/catchlightphotos   *www.linkedin.com/in/KimNagy*

Maryanne O'Hara

Maryanne O'Hara is the author of *Cascade*, the inaugural selection of *The Boston Globe* Book Club, a Massachusetts Book Award Fiction Honors winner, and a "pick" at *The Boston Globe*, *People*, *Slate* magazine, *Library Journal*, and others. She was the longtime associate fiction editor at Ploughshares and has had her short fiction widely published and anthologized. She is a graduate of Emerson College's MFA program, where she won the Graduate Dean's Award, and is the grateful recipient of grants from the St. Botolph Club Foundation and the Massachusetts Cultural Council.

www.maryanneohara.com

Neil A. O'Hara

Neil A. O'Hara is a freelance financial writer with intimate knowledge of domestic and international markets. His articles, written primarily for magazines aimed at professionals in the financial services industry, cover a wide range of subjects from hedge funds, private equity, and corporate governance to market and industry reviews as well as more technical topics, including exchange traded funds, credit derivatives, securities lending, prime brokerage, risk management, and financial industry regulations. He is also the author of record for the sixth edition of *The Fundamentals of Municipal Bonds* (John Wiley & Sons, 2011), an industry primer created by the Securities Industry and Financial Markets Association, and technical editor of the second edition of *Bond Investing for Dummies* (John Wiley & Sons, 2012). Before he became a professional writer in 2002, Mr. O'Hara worked in the financial services industry for more than twenty-eight years. Born and raised in England, Mr. O'Hara moved to New York in 1980 and became a naturalized American citizen in 2008. He has a bachelor of science degree in engineering and economics from the University of Warwick. An avid birdwatcher, he also enjoys hiking the trails in Lincoln, MA, where he lives with his wife, Katherine.

Katherine Hall Page

Katherine Hall Page is the author of twenty-two adult mysteries in the Faith Fairchild series, and five for younger readers. Among other honors, she received the Agatha for Best First (*The Body in the Belfry*), Best Novel (*The Body in the Snowdrift*), and Best Short Story ("The Would-Be Widower"). She has also published *Small Plates*, a short-story collection, and a series cookbook, *Have Faith in Your Kitchen*. A native of New Jersey, she has lived in Massachusetts since coming to college in 1965. Mount Auburn has always been a favorite destination, and appears most notably in her book, *The Body in the Attic*. Katherine and her husband live in Lincoln, MA.

www.katherine-hall-page.org

David Pallin

David Pallin is a retired senior banking executive with a primary interest in photography, and nature photography in particular. He found his interest in photography while earning a bachelor of arts degree from the University of Vermont and an MBA from New York University. He is the winner of the 2013 Mystic River Watershed Association Photo Contest. He and his family live in Winchester, MA.

Wayne R. Petersen

Wayne R. Petersen is director of the Massachusetts Important Bird Areas (IBA) Program at the Massachusetts Audubon Society. As co-author of *Birds of*

Massachusetts (1993) and co-editor of the *Massachusetts Breeding Bird Atlas* (2003) and the *Massachusetts Breeding Bird Atlas 2* (2013), his knowledge of the habitats, distribution, and status of the Commonwealth's bird life is both extensive and wide-ranging. A New England regional editor for *North American Birds* magazine and editor of the New England Christmas Bird Count, Wayne's knowledge of the seasonal distribution of New England bird life gives him a wide perspective when thinking about Important Bird Areas in Massachusetts and beyond. Among his other writing projects are authorship of the National Audubon Society's *Pocket Guide to Songbirds and Familiar Backyard Birds (East)* and *Birds of New England* (with Roger Burrows) and contributions to *The Audubon Society Master Guide to Birding*, *The Sibley Guide to Bird Life & Behavior*, and *Arctic Wings*. Wayne leads international birding tours for Mass Audubon, serves on the advisory committee of the Massachusetts Natural Heritage and Endangered Species Program and the Stellwagen Bank National Marine Sanctuary, and is a board member of the Wildlands Trust. In 2005 Wayne was the recipient of the American Birding Association's Ludlow Griscom Award for outstanding contributions in regional ornithology.

Mary Pinard

Mary Pinard teaches in the Arts and Humanities Division at Babson College. Her poems and essays have appeared in a variety of literary journals, and her book of poems, *Portal*, was published in 2014 by Salmon Press. She was born and raised in Seattle, WA.

Andy Provost

For about twenty years Andy Provost has been fortunate to photograph wildlife at Mount Auburn Cemetery, including hawks, owls, foxes, coyotes, and many migrating songbirds. He is grateful to Al Parker of the Mount Auburn staff who has been nice enough to call him when he finds critters (which is often because Al is one of the sharpest-eyed guys Andy knows). Yellowstone National Park and Florida are two yearly photo destinations for Andy, and Mount Auburn has been so productive that he refers to it as "Yellowstone East."

Jim Renault

Jim Renault has been enjoying amateur photography for over forty-five years, with a strong interest in wildlife and landscapes. In addition to photography, he enjoys astronomy, and often combines both hobbies into astrophotography. He grew up in Cambridge, MA, and currently lives in Arlington, MA, with his family. He is a graduate of Bentley University with a bachelor's degree in accounting.

Paul M. Roberts

Paul M. Roberts, of Medford, MA, was a corporate communications executive in the electronics industry for several decades. Paul began birding in 1971, and in 1976 founded the Eastern Massachusetts Hawk Watch, which he led for over twenty years. He served several years as editor of *Bird Observer*, was chair of the Hawk Migration Association of North America (HMANA) and still serves on their board, and has been president of the NorthEast Hawk Watch for over a decade. Paul received HMANA's highest lifetime honors, the Joseph Taylor and Maurice Brown awards, for his service to HMANA, hawk migration research, and raptor conservation. He lectures to bird clubs and teaches courses for Mass Audubon on hawks, shorebirds, and waterfowl. For the past ten years he has been researching and writing on Red-tailed Hawks in urban environments.

Hank Phillippi Ryan

Hank Phillipi Ryan is the on-air investigative reporter for Boston's NBC affiliate and also a bestselling author of seven mystery novels. She's won thirty-two Emmys, thirteen Edward R. Murrow Awards and dozens of other honors for her groundbreaking journalism. Her hard-hitting stories on such issues as mistakes in the 911 system that sent emergency responders to the wrong addresses, a failing jury selection system, firefighters given outmoded equipment, and corruption in the mortgage industry have changed laws and changed lives. Ryan has won multiple prestigious awards for her crime fiction: three Agathas; the Anthony, Daphne, and Macavity; and for *The Other Woman*, the coveted Mary Higgins Clark Award. National reviews have called her a "master at crafting suspenseful mysteries" and "a superb and gifted storyteller." Her 2013 novel, *The Wrong Girl*, had the extraordinary honor of winning the Agatha Award for Best Contemporary Novel and the Daphne Award for Mainstream Mystery/Suspense and was a seven-week Boston Globe bestseller. Her 2014 thriller, *Truth Be Told*, is an Agatha Award nominee for Best Mystery – a landmark back-to-back-to-back nomination – and was named a *Library Journal* Best Book of 2014. She was also nominated for the Agatha Award for Best Nonfiction as editor of the anthology of essays by mystery authors, *Writes of Passage*. Ryan's next novel in the continuing series, *What You See*, debuts in the fall of 2015. She's a founding teacher at Mystery Writers of America University and 2013 president of the national organization, Sisters in Crime.

Sandy Selesky

Sandy Selesky is the former building manager for the Center for European Studies at Harvard University. She retired in 2014 to devote more time to her photographic passion. As former president and now print coordinator at the Nashoba Valley Photo Club in Westford, MA, she has won numerous awards in New England and in international competitions, including the 2012 "Best of Show" award in the Glennie International Nature Salon. She is also a member of the invitation-only Camnats, a Massachusetts Camera Naturalists organization. She has had photographs in the following publications: *Nature Photographer* (including the Summer 2007 cover, plus over eight articles), *Nature's Best*, *Bird Observer*, *Birder's World*, *Wildlife Refuge Magazine* (including the Fall 2006 cover), and two U.S. Fish and Wildlife Service brochures. Her image, *Young,*

Wet, Great Horned Owl, was on exhibit at the Smithsonian Museum of Natural History in Washington, D.C., in spring 2006 along with other chosen winners of the Nature's Best International Photography Awards competition. Her image, *Black and White Warbler,* appeared on the cover of *Sweet Auburn* (the magazine of the Friends of Mount Auburn) for the Spring/Summer 2012 issue that celebrated the birds and birders of this historic cemetery.

Dan Shaughnessy

Dan Shaughnessy is a sports columnist for *The Boston Globe.* He was born in Groton, MA, graduated from Holy Cross, and worked at *The Evening Sun* (Baltimore) and *The Washington Star* from 1977-81. He joined *The Boston Globe* in 1981, and has been a sports columnist since 1989. He has been named Massachusetts Sportswriter of the Year eleven times, and has been voted one of America's top-ten sports columnists ten times by the Associated Press Sports Editors. Shaughnessy has written twelve books, including The New York Times Best Seller, *Francona; The Curse of the Bambino;* and *Senior Year.* He makes regular appearances on *The SportsHub,* 98.5 FM; WHDH's *SportsXtra;* and Comcast's *Sports New England.* He is married to Dr. Marilou Shaughnessy and lives in Newton, MA.

David Sibley

David Sibley, son of ornithologist Fred Sibley, began seriously watching and drawing birds in 1969, at age seven. Since 1980 David has traveled throughout the North American continent in search of birds, both on his own and as a leader of birdwatching tours, and has lived in California, Arizona, Texas, Florida, Georgia, New York, Connecticut, and New Jersey. This intensive travel and bird study culminated in the publication of his comprehensive guide to bird identification – *The Sibley Guide to Birds* – in the fall of 2000, and the completely updated second edition in 2014. Other books include a companion volume – *The Sibley Guide to Bird Life & Behavior* – in the fall of 2001, *Sibley's Birding Basics* – an introduction to bird identification – in 2002, and the *Sibley Field Guides to Eastern and Western Birds* in 2003. In 2009 he completed a fully illustrated guide to the identification of North American trees – *The Sibley Guide to Trees.* He is the recipient of the Roger Tory Peterson Award for lifetime achievement from the American Birding Association and the Linnaean Society of New York's Eisenmann Medal. David now lives in Concord, MA, where he continues to study and draw birds and trees. A lot of the field work for *The Sibley Guide to Trees* was done in Mount Auburn Cemetery, and David enjoys birding there at all seasons.

www.sibleyguides.com

Eric Smith

Eric Smith grew up in Massachusetts behind an Audubon sanctuary and spent most afternoons playing outdoors. That love of nature developed into becoming a birder and then a wildlife photographer. He's lucky enough to live not too far from Mount Auburn and loves to go there all year long. The Dell is his favorite place there – he loves to watch the Great Horned Owls, and one migration weekend he reveled in watching two Canada Warblers bathing in the Dell's pond while watching four more waiting in the bushes to take their turn. From coyote in the winter to colorful migrants in the spring and yearlong residents, there is always something interesting in Mount Auburn. Eric is on the board of the Eastern Massachusetts Hawk Watch and the Menotomy Bird Club, and he teaches digital photography for Mass Audubon. When not at home in Waltham, MA, he can be found most weekends exploring the wilds of New England.

Phil Sorrentino

Phil Sorrentino is a chemical engineer who lived in Belmont, quite close to Mount Auburn Cemetery, until moving recently to Southborough, MA, with his wife Jennifer and son Jack. He enjoys all aspects of nature and wildlife photography, but has special regard for shooting birds of prey and warblers in Mount Auburn.

Leslie Wheeler

Leslie Wheeler is an award-winning author of books about American history and biographies. *Loving Warriors,* her biography in letters of the nineteenth-century feminist Lucy Stone and her husband, Henry Blackwell, won the English Speaking Union's Ambassador of Honor Award as an "outstanding interpreter of American life and history." She is also the author of the Miranda Lewis "living history" mystery series, and is a co-editor/publisher at Level Best Books, which publishes an annual anthology of crime stories by New England authors. A member of Mystery Writers of America and Sisters in Crime, Leslie serves as speakers bureau coordinator for the New England chapter, and is a founding member of the New England Crime Bake Committee.

www.lesliewheeler.com

Robin feeding chicks. Photo by Kim Nagy.